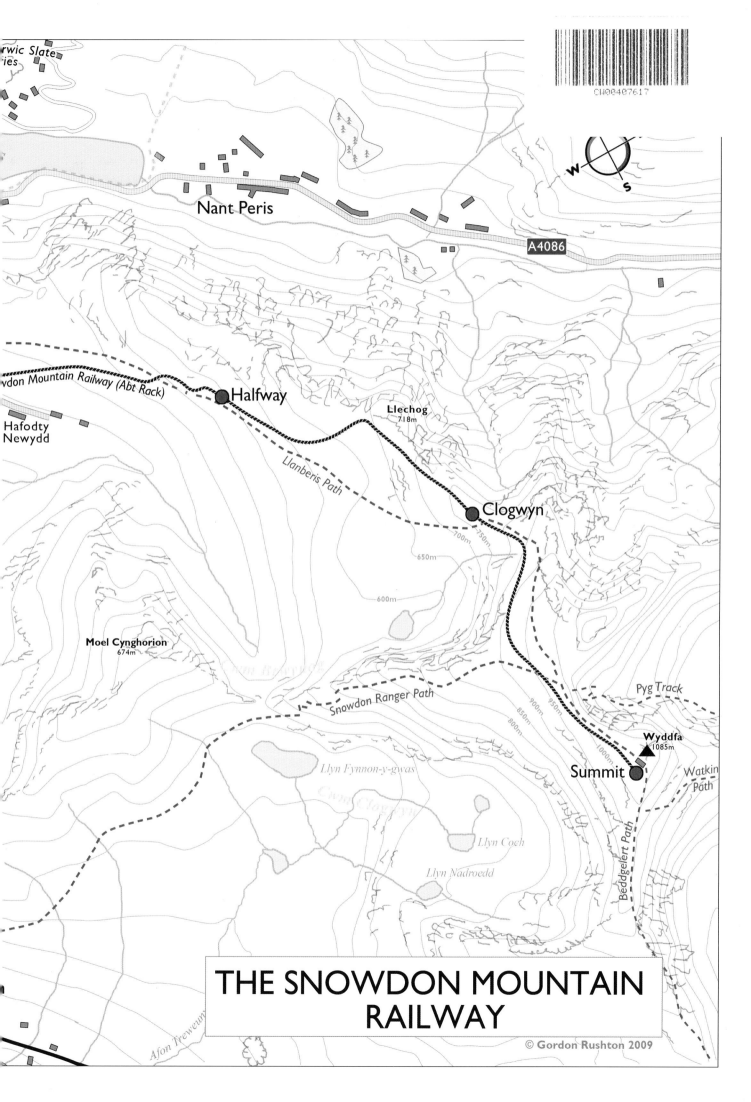

THE SNOWDON MOUNTAIN RAILWAY

An Illustrated History of the
Snowdon Mountain Railway

An Illustrated History of the

Snowdon Mountain Railway

Peter Johnson

An imprint of
Ian Allan Publishing

First published 2010

ISBN 978 0 86093 613 2

Published by Ian Allan Publishing

an imprint of Ian Allan Publishing Ltd, Hersham, Surrey KT12 4RG. Printed in England by Ian Allan Printing Ltd, Hersham, Surrey KT12 4RG.

Visit the Ian Allan Publishing website at www.ianallanpublishing.com

Distributed in the Unites States of America and Canada by BookMasters Distribution Services.

Code: 1004/B3

Mixed Sources
Product group from well-managed forests and other controlled sources
www.fsc.org Cert no. SGS-COC-005526
© 1996 Forest Stewardship Council
FSC

Front cover: **On 21 June 1996, the day the railway celebrated its centenary, No 4** *Snowdon* **approaches the summit.** *Author*

Title page: **No 5** *Moel Siabod* **and its carriage at Llanberis shortly after delivery in 1896.** *Author's collection*

Half title: **No 2** *Enid* **returns to Llanberis, near Hebron in June 1976.** *Alan Bowler*

Below: **A new logo was introduced by the current regime, 14 April 2001.**

Right: **Shortly after opening No 3 and its carriage were seen near the summit. The passengers' demeanour indicates that they were aware of the photographer's presence. The photograph shows the home signal and the telegraph posts and wires.**
Commercial postcard/Author's collection

Crown copyright is reserved for illustrations from the National Archives and the Ordnance Survey.

Unattributed photographs post-1970 taken by the author

Contents

Introduction

For many visitors to North Wales a trip to Llanberis to travel on the Snowdon Mountain Railway is a 'must do'. A Swiss mountain railway climbing to the summit of Snowdon, which at 3,560ft is the highest mountain in England and Wales, it remains a unique public railway in the United Kingdom.

The railway is also exceptional in that it was the first in the United Kingdom to be built with the carriage of tourists as its primary objective, any ambitions its promoters had to carry goods being quickly forgotten. Furthermore, it is one of a very small number of non-statutory passenger-carrying railways, built without legal authority; the Fairbourne Railway and the 15in gauge Ravenglass & Eskdale Railway are other examples.

During the 19th century, the village of Llanberis developed from being a centre for the quarrymen working at the nearby Dinorwic quarries to becoming also a centre for the burgeoning middle-class tourism industry, particularly to accommodate an increasing demand for guided tours to the summit of Snowdon.

Early proposals to build a railway there were rebuffed by the landowner, but the situation changed after the North Wales Narrow Gauge Railways renamed its Rhyd Ddu terminal station Snowdon in 1893, and took most of the tourist traffic to the other side of the mountain. The landowner, anxious to protect the livelihoods of his tenants in Llanberis, agreed to a railway being built.

The events of the first day in 1896 are well known; the derailment and loss of a locomotive, the passenger jumping off and fatally injuring himself, followed by a collision in low cloud. The railway made the headlines in a way that must have been most unsettling for the directors and investors. However, the railway recovered, was re-opened and settled down to become a feature of both the landscape and the tourists' agenda.

In 1922, a new board of directors took over, bringing the railway under the control of the same team then running the Festiniog Railway and responsible for promoting the Welsh Highland Railway. Under new management, the railway's traffic was expanded and it was to pay regular dividends to its shareholders for the first time. The involvement of Evan R. Davies as one of the new directors was to be continued after his death in 1934, via his brother, sons and grandchildren, until 1999.

From 1939, the Second World War brought with it restrictions of access to the mountain and to train operating, especially after various government agencies took control of the summit building. The track, which had never been renewed, was in poor condition when passenger services were resumed after the war and the railway's operating practices brought it to the attention of the railway inspectors. A programme of track repairs and the introduction of new operating procedures led to a new era of financial success.

In 1984, control of the company passed to a property company. Capital restructuring followed by a share issue brought with them a new regime of expansion with the acquisition of a fleet of modern purpose-built diesel locomotives and railcars.

A further change of control in 1998 placed the railway in a group owning other tourist attractions and led to the original company being made private in 1999.

The 21st century world is very different to that of the 19th century when the Snowdon Mountain Railway was constructed, but it still has a part to play in giving the public access to some of Wales's most splendid scenery.

Acknowledgements

The commissioning of this book followed an encounter between Alan Kendall, the SMR's general manager, and myself on the Ffestiniog Railway on 22 May 2007, when the FR celebrated the 175th anniversary of its act of Parliament. The link is fortuitous, for from 1921 until 1954 the two railways, and the Welsh Highland Railway until it was placed in liquidation, were in common ownership. One of the key figures of that period was Evan Robert Davies, whose family remained involved with the SMR until 1999.

I met Ninian Rhys Davies, one of his Davies's sons and then SMR company chairman, when I first wrote about the railway some 20 years ago, a feature for the now-defunct Railway World magazine.

In connection with this book, I was pleased to meet Ninian Davies's daughter Gillian, a one-time director of the SMR. She recalled family memories about the railway and produced photographs and other documents in her collection. She also gave me an introduction to her brother Andrew's widow, Meg Davies. Andrew Davies had been an SMR director too, and despite a recent house move Meg was able to find correspondence dealing with the 1984 sale of the railway and a significant number of photographs. She remembered Andrew telling her how he spent a few weeks as an SMR fireman when he was a young man.

I met the late general manager, Derek Rogerson, when I met Ninian Davies, keeping in contact with him until he retired in 1996. Some of the information that he gave me and reproduced herein was first published in the Railway World article.

Derek's successor, Tony Hopkins, has been kind enough to respond to questions dealing with the period of his management. He also helped me to make contact with Gillian Davies. Information given to me by both Derek and Tony and published in the narrow gauge railway news columns that I contributed to *Railway World* from 1991 until 1995, and to *Steam Railway* magazine from 1995 has also been useful here. I enjoyed Tony's company, and that of his wife Sue, during a journey to view the new summit building on the day that it was opened, 12 June 2009.

David Crowe, son of SMR director Norman Ronald Aubrey Crowe, was found via the internet. An SMR shareholder thanks to a bequest from Charlotte Pauline Macinnes, widow of Henry Jack Macinnes, originally Henry Joseph Jack, he tracked down a photograph of his father and produced his SMR share certificate, remembering that he bought his first car with the income tax reclaimed on SMR dividends.

Nigel Ross, formerly of Cadogan, the company that controlled the SMR from 1984 until 1998, and who was chairman from 1989 until 1998, told me how he became aware of the SMR and the reasons behind its disposal.

In addition to Alan Kendall, I am indebted to his staff for their enthusiastic support during this project. Judith Pettit, with whom I had competed for SMR material on eBay, kindly made her postcard collection available. Senior engineering manager Doug Blair supplied photographs and gave me an insight into the imaginative 21st century technical solutions employed by the 19th century railway.

Tony Ellis, who I first knew as an SMR controller during the 1990s, has a long-standing interest in its history. He worked on the railway for 47 years. His father worked on the SMR and his grandfather was employed by the company in 1896. Over the years he has acquired historical material which was being thrown out, and kindly made it available to me.

When I told my Ffestiniog Railway friend Rob Smallman that I was to write this book he told me how his grandparents had been honeymooning in Llandudno in April 1896 and managed to ride on the first train, avoiding the accident because they walked back to Llanberis. When I asked him if the Frederic Smallman listed as a £200 debenture holder in 1895 could be a relative, he replied that his middle name is Frederic. The investment must explain how Frederic was able to secure places on the first train.

Photographically, the SMR is rather strange. After the opening, the pool of photographs is very small. Of the hundreds of picture postcards that must exist, most suffer from being poorly printed and the majority were taken near the summit so tend to duplicate each other. There are also many aspects of the SMR that escaped the camera, No 6 running in 1922 with its original name, *Sir Harmood*, for example. Considering that the railway is a tourist attraction, and compared with other railways in the locality, there are very few photographs taken in the 1920s and 1930s, when people started to take holidays accompanied by a Kodak box Brownie or similar. There are fewer pre-war enthusiast pictures than might be expected, as well.

That said, it has been possible to turn up some historical photographs that have not been published either before or recently. The SMR kindly made its own small archive available and for more recent photographs I must thank Alan Bowler, Hugh Ballantyne, Andrew Hurrill and John Kenward. Glyn Jones, a seasonal employee with the SMR in the 1960s and now resident in the USA, gave me copies of his SMR ephemera. Michael Bishop made Donovan Box's photographs available. Edward Dorricott supplied photographs and loaned me his ephemera collection. John Allsop supplied scans of more than 100 postcards and photographs from his collection. John Keylock and David Allan of the Welsh Highland Railway Heritage Group kindly made the photograph of Henry Joseph

Jack available. Gillian Davies supplied photographs of most of her railway-connected relatives and some otherwise unseen postcards. Meg Davies's collection included photographs that had been submitted for a competition in 1933; some of which featured the interior of the 1935 summit building.

Historically, whilst always proud of its heritage, the SMR did not appear to recognise the significance of its archive. Documents rescued by Tony Ellis in the course of its being thrown out indicates the scale of the lost material: Aitchison's correspondence and reports dealing with the SMTH, the North Wales Narrow Gauge Railways, the Portmadoc, Beddgelert & South Snowdon Railway and the North Wales Power & Traction Company; Owen's correspondence and reports relating to the SMTH/SMR, and Festiniog Railway and Welsh Highland Railway from the 1920s and 1930s. The present management has deposited material with the Gwynedd Archives at Caernarfon that is not yet open to public access. The material it retains, Fox's construction contract book, three out of four minute books covering the period 1895 to 1960, and some correspondence from the 1920s, was made available to me and I am grateful for that.

Adrian Gray, the Festiniog Railway's archivist, and Patricia Ward made it possible for me to see Spooner's 1877 report to the FR directors concerning his proposal for a railway from Portmadoc to the summit of Snowdon. It had been in a private collection that had been transferred to the FR's Archives just a few weeks before I saw it. Adrian also made available the SMR enamel sign for photography.

Not being a statutory railway company, the SMR was not required to make returns to the Board of Trade so there are no records of passengers carried, train mileage, or a breakdown of receipts and expenditure that are available for statutory lines. Michael Bishop directed me towards the City of London Corporation's Guildhall Library as the repository for company reports deposited with the Stock Exchange prior to 1964. However, although I saw most of the SMR's reports there, the early reports contained only the minimum information required under company legislation. Companies House supplied copies of reports from 1973 until 2002 on microfiche and more recent ones via the internet.

Despite the limitations of its official records, there are files dealing with the SMR in the National Archives at Kew. They deal with the 1896 inspection, the accident and its aftermath, a proposed agreement with the Air Ministry in 1942/3 and the post-war complaints that led to the introduction of the military railway train control system.

The British Telecom archive in High Holborn has a file dealing with the establishment of the public telegraph station at the summit. The National Trust records at the Gwynedd Archives contain deeds and plans of the land owned by the SMR in the Aberglaslyn Pass. Plans of the pre-SMR schemes were viewed at the House of Lords Records Office. Contemporary railway and engineering magazines were viewed at the University of Leicester's David Wilson Library.

The internet gave access to the digital archives of the *Times* and the *Manchester Guardian* and the 49 newspapers in the British Library's 19th century newspaper collection. Microfilm of the *North Wales Chronicle* and the *Carnarvon & Denbigh Herald* were viewed at the British Library's newspaper library at Colindale.

It seems appropriate that a technical description of the SMR (Appendix 1) should use the words of its first manager, Gowrie Colquhoun Aitchison. He played a significant part in the SMR's development in addition to being employed by the North Wales Narrow Gauge Railways, the North Wales Power

& Traction Company and the Portmadoc, Beddgelert & South Snowdon Railway.

While writing this book I realised that I was unwittingly completing a trilogy about the railways run by Evan R. Davies and Henry Joseph Jack, the others being the Festiniog and Welsh Highland. Despite learning much about what they did, I am still no further forward in discovering how their partner and source of finance, Sir John Henderson Stewart Bt, became involved.

Delving into the sources mentioned has been a journey of discovery and I uncovered much more about the Snowdon Mountain Railway than I ever imagined possible. It is my pleasure to share my knowledge with a wider audience.

Adrian Gray and Tony Hopkins read the draft text and I am grateful for their insights. Any opinions expressed are my own and I accept responsibility for any errors.

Peter Johnson
Leicester
February 2010

A logo used by the railway on printed matter during the inter-war years. *Author's collection*

Miscellenea

Welsh place names

During most of the period covered by this book many Welsh place names were anglicised. Over the last 40 years or so the Welsh forms have been restored. The archaic forms are used here where most appropriate. For clarification the places concerned are:

Bettws y Coed = Betws y Coed
Carnarvon/Caernarvon = Caernarfon
Portmadoc = Porthmadog
Quellyn = Cwellyn.

Abbreviations

FR	Festiniog/Ffestiniog Railway
HRCNW	Hotels & Railway Company of North Wales
LNWR	London & North Western Railway
LMSR	London, Midland & Scottish Railway
NWNGR	North Wales Narrow Gauge Railways
NWPT	North Wales Power & Traction Company
PBSSR	Portmadoc, Beddgelert & South Snowdon Railway
SLM	Société Suisse pour la Construction de Locomotives et de Machines; Schweizerische Locomotiv & Maschinenfabrik; Swiss Locomotive Company
SMR	Snowdon Mountain Railway
SMTH	Snowdon Mountain Tramroad & Hotels Company
SNPA	Snowdonia National Park Authority
WHR	Welsh Highland Railway

Currency and distance

£1 = 240d (pence) = 20s (shillings);
1s = 12d;
£1 guinea = £1 1s.

1 Mile = 1,760 yards
22 Yards = 1 chain

The value of money
Equivalent value of £1 in 2009

1890	£59.89
1900	£57.06
1905	£57.35
1910	£57.06
1915	£43.06
1920	£21.21
1925	£29.97
1930	£33.42
1935	£36.98
1940	£28.72
1945	£25.95
1950	£22.78
1955	£17.42
1960	£15.30

Data extracted from the currency converter on the National Archives website: **www.nationalarchives.gov.uk/currency/**

Preliminaries and cutting the first sod

In the early 19th century, the Carnarvonshire village of Llanberis, with a population of fewer than 500 and 348ft above sea level, was largely dependent on the nearby Dinorwic slate quarries for employment. It is located at the south eastern end of Llyn Padarn, or Llanberis Lake, a natural feature some two miles long. It is also at the foot of the north face of Snowdon, the highest mountain in England and Wales, 3,560ft above sea level, and the start of the easiest walking route to the summit. In Welsh, the mountain is Yr Wyddfa or Eryri, the former meaning tomb or monument in reference to a mythological tomb, and the latter meaning Snowdonia.

Thomas Pennant's account of his tour of Wales, published in 1781, is attributed as having started tourism to Llanberis, with Snowdon's summit as the objective. Guiding visitors thence, either on foot or on horseback, became a worthwhile occupation that contributed to the prosperity of the village. Improved access to the area following the opening of Telford's Holyhead road in 1815 brought more visitors.

The summit of Snowdon – a view probably dating from the late 17th century. This engraving not only lacks perspective but shows a veritable highway to the Snowdon summit. *Newman & Company/ Author's collection*

The arrival of the railway at Bangor in 1848 and at Carnarvon in 1852 was followed by the construction of a branch from the latter to Llanberis in 1869, all improving access for visitors. It was at the opening of the last that Sir Richard Moon, then chairman of the London & North Western Railway (LNWR), suggested that Snowdon had to be the next target for a railway. Bills deposited in Parliament in 1871 and 1874 were rejected owing to opposition from the landowner, George William Duff Assheton-Smith. Beneficiary of the Vaynol estate, he owned much of the land in the locality, including the Dinorwic quarries. Both of the 1870s schemes terminated near Clogwyn, a good hike away from the summit, unlike the line that was eventually built.

Another rail option for visitors to the mountain was the North Wales Narrow Gauge Railway's Moel Tryfan undertaking, opened to Rhyd Ddu, on the mountain's south-western flank in 1881. The station was promoted as the 'closest to the summit of Snowdon'. The NWNGR's renaming of Rhyd Ddu station as Snowdon in 1893 led to a big increase in passenger numbers on that railway and a serious loss of business in Llanberis. On 22 December 1894, the *Railway News* was to attribute the decline of Llanberis to tipping slate waste from Glynrhonwy into the lake and to Sir Edward Watkin's path to the summit, which started from the Nant Gwynant side of Beddgelert and opened in 1892, as well as the facilities provided by the NWNGR.

In 1877, Charles Easton Spooner, then the Festiniog Railway's secretary and engineer, tried to interest the FR directors in promoting a railway from Portmadoc, via the Croesor Tramway, Beddgelert and Rhyd Ddu, to the summit of Snowdon. In 1896 John Sylvester Hughes was to say, in the *North Wales Chronicle*, that he and Spooner had surveyed a route that had continued to Llanberis. The sketch that accompanied Spooner's report was obviously not the result of a survey so the route that Hughes wrote about must have been another proposal.

Even without Assheton-Smith's objection to these schemes, any parliamentary proposal might well have failed because it was not for nearly another 100 years that the development of railways for tourism was considered to be in the public interest.

By time of the 1891 census, Llanberis's population was 2,818, having peaked at 3,033 in 1881, most of the growth undoubtedly owing to expansion at the quarries. There was sufficient concern, however, about the impact on villagers' lives caused by the reduction in visitor numbers for Assheton-Smith's agent, Captain N. P. Stewart, to press for a railway to the summit of Snowdon.

His efforts began to be rewarded in 1894. Sir Douglas Fox and his brother Francis were chosen as the project's engineers and their Frank Oswell made a preliminary survey in May.

By October 1894 stories about a proposed railway to the summit had circulated sufficiently for Canon Hardwick D. Rawnsley, the secretary of the newly formed National Trust for the Preservation of Sites of Historical Interest and National Beauty, to write to Stewart to ask if there was any truth in the rumours, claiming that 'a large number of people in all parts of the United Kingdom are alarmed … They fear that if once the interest of the railway engineer or hotel proprietor are allowed on such a mountain as Snowdon to outweigh the best interests of the lovers of our native land undisfigured and undestroyed there will be an end to all real enjoyment of mountain scenery throughout the country. The deplorable example set on Snowdon will touch every mountain height…' What was acceptable in Italy and Switzerland, where the heat of the plains and valleys encouraged development in the mountains, 'would seem to be hardly necessary or practicable in our own climate.' Stewart replied that although a line had been surveyed he could not say 'to a certainty' that it would be built and pointed out that Assheton-Smith was not promoting the scheme but was granting facilities to others.

He continued: 'But, assuming that a railway is made, I do not see that this need deprive mountain climbers of their climb. They can have their climb all the same, if they prefer it to be being whisked to the summit by steam or electricity. Don't you think on reflection, however, that the view you take of the matter is rather selfish? Why should Mr Assheton-Smith be debarred from promoting the interests and prosperity of the people amongst whom he dwells? Why should Snowdon be reserved exclusively for the enjoyment of mountain climbers? Why should they have the entire monopoly of the mountain? Are there not thousands and tens of thousands of people, some too young and some too old and others who from various causes find themselves unable to make the ascent who would like to inhale the exhilarating air of the mountain and from the highest summit in England or Wales look down on the glorious panorama that lies beneath? Is not the greatest happiness of the greatest number the true end to be achieved? And is not he who lends a hand in this direction a benefactor of this country?'

Writing on 23 October, Rawnsley acknowledged that Stewart's reply was courteous before attacking Assheton-Smith for agreeing 'to this objectionable scheme of vulgarising one of our grandest natural possessions.' He was still hoping that Assheton-Smith would see that 'Snowdon, unvulgarised and uncommercialised, is, after all, the best investment for "a declining Llanberis," and may believe that it is no selfish spirit but a real love of our country and a real belief in the growth of the appreciation of nature among the people that would urge him at the eleventh hour to refuse to others the "reasonable facilities" to which he is really opposed and of which he has refused to avail himself' before concluding: '... It seems to me, though, of course, it is only my opinion, that anyone who will deprive the people of the chief joy of such an ascent by taking away all the association with mountain solitude, as will be done the moment a railway and its accompaniments are imported to the scene, is directly taking away the greatest happiness of the greatest number for the sake of the profit to the few, and he who

lends a hand in this direction can surely in no sense claim to be a benefactor of his country.'

On 1 November Stewart replied: '... I am glad you acknowledge my letter to have been a courteous one, and regret to discover so little of that quality in yours. When you find yourself defeated in argument you indulge in sentiment, and I can only regard your epistles as the sulky, sentimental dribble (canonised) of a dreamer and faddist. I must ask you not to trouble me with further communications.'

In fact, Rawnsley had already gone over Stewart's head by writing to Assheton-Smith on 23 October: '... if it could be shown you that the preponderant sense of the nation were against such innovation, you would take firm steps to prevent so sacred an inheritance as Snowdon being thus robbed of its chief charm for future generations, and vulgarised forever.' Suggesting that developments on Snowdon would set a precedent for other mountains in the UK he went on to appeal to Assheton-Smith's sense of patriotism, concluding: 'It is in very few places in our crowded country that man can be alone with nature, and with their God – and Snowdon is one of them. To rob Snowdon, so easily accessible as it is both by night and by day, of its grand natural solitude and super eminent charm will be to inflict a loss upon the whole world.'

Below left: **The proposed Snowdon Railway Company route of 1872. It would have been 4 miles 1 furlong 6 chains long, running from the site of the 1896 railway and terminating 35 chains (770yd) from the public house at the summit. The only named promoter was John McMillan John Wilkinson. Engineer Eugene Birch signed the construction estimate of £20,337 16s.** *HLRO*

Below: **A second Snowdon bill was deposited in November 1874. The proposed route would have followed a similar, but not identical, route to the 1872 proposal and terminated 900yd from the summit. On 9 January 1875, the *Graphic* reported that it was intended to be a Rigi railway but on 30 January 1875 the *North Wales Chronicle* reported that the bill had been withdrawn.** *HLRO*

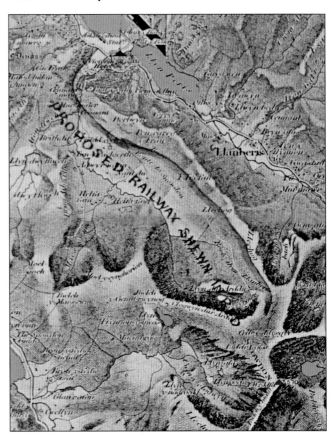

To which Assheton-Smith answered: 'I regret to say that I cannot take the same view of the matter as your association appears to do. You are right in saying that I was in former years opposed to the scheme; but times have changed, and if in many ways one does not advance with them, one is left alone. In trying to direct the tourists to Llanberis, and making things easy for them, I am consulting the interest of the estate and the neighbourhood in which I live, and I cannot recognise any outside interference in the matter.'

Ratcheting up the pressure, Rawnsley responded on 27 October: '… I felt from what I had heard that you had at last, in your kindness, given way to certain local representations, and that probably in heart you were opposed as ever to the scheme. Knowing that many of my fellow-countrymen, from no selfish spirit, are strongly opposed to the introduction into our land of the Swiss mountain-railway craze, with its utter destruction of one of the chief charms of mountain scenery for all future time, and feeling that the interest in preserving Snowdon from such harm was more than local, I venture to approach you. I hope you will have no objection to our correspondence being made public.'

On 6 November the *Times* published a letter from Rawnsley that included his correspondence with Assheton-Smith, Rawnsley concluding that there was no need for the railway. The mountain was already accessible to all but the infirm, and the 'little refreshment house on the summit, with its four beds probably satisfies the needs of those who wish to see the sun rise'. He agreed that the railway would be good for Llanberis but at the expense of the existing guides and the other villages used to make the ascent. They, he cited Beddgelert and Capel Curig, might then promote their own railways to the summit. Swiss mountain railways demonstrated that there would be no cheap fares so the railway would only benefit the 'well to do'. As the tourist season was so short the only way that the railway could cover its operating costs would be by exploiting the mountain for mineral traffic. 'Those who remember what Llanberis was before the quarries existed, are naturally not anxious to see the Llanberis experiment repeated …'

His greatest objection, however, remained what he called the 'commercialising of scenery.' 'Snowdon unrailwayed, unvulgarised, and unexploited,' he said, 'is a better investment for Wales, for Llanberis … than Snowdon turned into a mixture of tea-garden and switchback.' 'The love of natural scenery – ' he continued, 'hardly more than a century old in Great Britain – is working gradually downward into the mass of the people; and the inevitable crowding into the cities, with all the accompaniment of train and tram, as inevitably makes men desire more and more something that is without these accompaniments for their rest and enjoyment.' He closed by referring to the Lake District, where 'within the past few years the claims of natural scenery have been held by Parliament to be superior to the claims of the railway promoter's pocket …'

The *Times* published a reply from Stewart on 9 November in which he pointed out that Rawnsley had been in correspondence with him and had only released half of the correspondence with the Vaynol estate, saying: 'The rev gentleman considered it necessary to supplement the letters by a lengthy disquisition setting forth his own particular views. I refrain from following his lead in this respect, and content myself with merely supplying you with copies of the correspondence, and leave it to your readers to form their own conclusions.' In a postscript he added that Rawnsley was ill-informed about Snowdon, saying that it was not uncommon for 500 people to ascend the mountain in a day and that on one day earlier in the year more than 1,000 had reached the summit.

Left: **Looking from Llanberis, the Victoria Hotel is prominent, centre, in this 1865 photograph. The roof of the building now occupied by the SMR's offices is visible on the right.** *H. Petschler/ Author's collection*

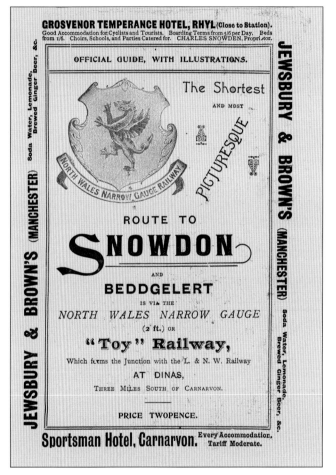

The cover of a North Wales Narrow Gauge Railways' guide promoting it as the 'shortest and most picturesque route to Snowdon'. *Author's collection*

The exchange was repeated in other newspapers. In the *Times* it attracted support for the railway from Robert St John Corbet of Shrewsbury, saying: 'Only one side of the giant hill would be disfigured' and 'a cultured man like Canon Rawnsley … need [not] fear anything from the multiplication of excursionists, male and female, learned and ignorant, serious and frivolous.'

Commenting on the *Times* correspondence, the *Manchester Guardian's* Welsh correspondent, published on 13 November, was critical of the railway, saying: 'If Welshmen have a spark of genuine patriotism in them they will rise as one man against this "desecration" as it may well be called, of the grandest natural feature of their country … I shall be much disappointed if Welshmen will allow a commercial enterprise to ruin the charms of the most glorious of all their mountains.'

The editor of the *North Wales Chronicle*, writing on 17 November, also commented on the dispute. 'The action of Mr Assheton-Smith in granting facilities ... has called forth the indignant protest of the secretary ... and the usual aesthetic persons always ready to join a newspaper correspondence, which may serve to exhibit their "superiority" ... the secretary had all the facts before him when he first lifted up his voice against the so-called desecration of Snowdon, but those facts seemed to have no effect whatever upon the reverend gentleman, whose sense of beauty is apparently out of all proportion to what ordinary folks would call common sense. It is always an easy matter to pose as a champion of the preservation of natural beauty, but the fact that the sympathy of unthinking people is enlisted with ease should be a caution to plain men to be quite sure that there is really a good case before any question of desecration or vandalism is publicly raised. We venture to think that if Canon Rawnsley had tempered his platitudes with a little respect for common sense and a regard for facts, he would not have failed to appreciate the kindness which prompted Mr Assheton-Smith and his advisers to grant facilities for the construction of the proposed Snowdon Railway... Had Mr Assheton-Smith turned a deaf ear to the petitions of his people, the radical and socialist press, which is now filled with shrieking denunciations of the desecration of Snowdon, would not have ceased from holding up to obloquy the landlord who preferred his own sentimental fancy to the prosperity of the thousands who inhabit Llanberis.

'The people who live in the Snowdon district have no need to be told that it is no unusual sight in summer to see long trains crowded with tourists going in the direction of Snowdon, but it is equally well known that, by a clever device of the promoters of the narrow gauge railway, the stream of visitors has been almost entirely diverted from Llanberis. The re-christening of the Rhyd Ddu terminus and calling it Snowdon attracts thousands of tourists annually, with loss to the lodging house keepers, hotel keepers, and the general population of Llanberis. As Captain Stewart pointed out ... it is absurd folly to speak of the solitudes of Snowdon during the summer months, and it is equally silly to describe the people who make the ascent as 'bun and whisky' tourists. As a matter of fact the crowds that visit Snowdon are ordinary and decent people ... It is therefore under a sense of what he owes to the people of Llanberis, Mr Assheton Smith withdraws his opposition to the scheme, from which he derives no benefit whatever.'

Obviously the editor of a North Wales newspaper was not going to criticise the Vaynol estate. A council member of the National Society for Checking the Abuses of Public Advertising added to the *Times'* correspondence on 19 November by taking a different stance, saying that the real issue was not with the railway itself but with 'the perfectly gratuitous disfigurements which it is generally allowed to bring in its train.' 'Let, then,' he continued, 'those who would if they could keep Snowdon as it is reserve some part of their energy for securing that the intrusion of the locomotive shall do the least possible harm to the amenities. They can, if they chose to concentrate their energies, make it a condition that neither the stations nor the line shall be used for puffing disfigurements; that the buildings and all else shall be modest, and not unnecessarily out of keeping with the scene ... There is really no reason why places where meat and drink are dispensed should cause offence. I admit that they generally do, but that is because people take it for granted that they must. But, if need were, I could mention instances where much-frequented hostelries have been not merely useful, but perfectly harmless, additions to fine scenery.' The society had been formed in 1893 and was to play a part in securing the 1907 Advertisements Regulation Act; the designer and socialist William Morris was a member.

The president of the Board of Trade, James Bryce MP, addressing members of the Norwegian Club on 11 December declared that he wished that he had the power to 'check the attempt to make a railway to the top of Snowdon.' The first sod was cut on 15 December 1894.

Earlier, on 24 November, the *North Wales Chronicle* had published a brief statement to the effect that the first sod ceremony of the 'Snowdon Electric Railway' set for 5 December had been deferred to the later date.

To build and operate the railway a company, the Snowdon Mountain Tramroad & Hotels Company Ltd (SMTH), had been incorporated under the Companies Acts 1862-90 on 16 November 1894. The company's registered office was at the Victoria Hotel, Llanberis. Its objects were quite wide-ranging but principally 'to construct a tramroad from Llanberis ... to a point at or near the summit of Snowdon, in the parish of Beddgelert ... and to erect an [sic] hotel at or near the summit'; to enter into agreements; to construct extensions to the tramroad, and other tramroads, tramways or railways in Great Britain, and lines of telegraph or telephone wires and other works; to maintain and work and carry on the tramroads, tramways or railways and to carry on the business of carriers of passengers and goods 'by land or water'; 'to carry on the Victoria Hotel ... and the hotel proposed ... and any other hotels in Great Britain...' The share capital was £70,000 in £10 shares.

The original subscribers were: Wallace William Cragg, Lieutenant Colonel; George Holme, architect; Frederick Morton Radcliffe, solicitor; Henry Cottingham Nicholson,

A NWNGR advertisement encouraging tourist traffic to Snowdon and Beddgelert, via Rhyd Ddu, the station renamed Snowdon in 1893. *Author's collection*

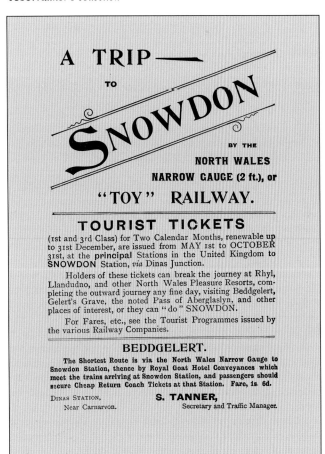

A TRIP —
TO
SNOWDON
BY THE
NORTH WALES
NARROW GAUGE (2 ft.), or
"TOY" RAILWAY.

TOURIST TICKETS

(1st and 3rd Class) for Two Calendar Months, renewable up to 31st December, are issued from MAY 1st to OCTOBER 31st, at the **principal** Stations in the United Kingdom to SNOWDON Station, *via* Dinas Junction.

Holders of these tickets can break the journey at Rhyl, Llandudno, and other North Wales Pleasure Resorts, completing the outward journey any fine day, visiting Beddgelert, Gelert's Grave, the noted Pass of Aberglaslyn, and other places of interest, or they can "do" SNOWDON.

For Fares, etc., see the Tourist Programmes issued by the various Railway Companies.

BEDDGELERT.

The Shortest Route is via the North Wales Narrow Gauge to Snowdon Station, thence by Royal Goat Hotel Conveyances which meet the trains arriving at Snowdon Station, and passengers should secure Cheap Return Coach Tickets at that Station. Fare, 1s. 6d.

DINAS STATION, **S. TANNER,**
Near Carnarvon. Secretary and Traffic Manager.

stock and share broker; J. H. Welsford, shipowner; Harry Clegg, esquire, and Frank W. Turner, gentleman. Only the last two had local connections, the others being from, or based in, Liverpool.

Two agreements were specified in the company's articles, the first with the Hotels & Railway Company of North Wales Ltd (HRCNW), the second with Arthur Hill Holme and Charles Wilden King, the Liverpool-based contractors.

HRCNW appears to have been a special vehicle set up to transfer Assheton-Smith/Vaynol estate property to SMTH. A preliminary agreement made on 15 October 1894 provided for the sale of the land required for the railway by the trustees of the Vaynol estate to Cragg, or to a company to be formed by him, for £1,500, and for the lease to him of the Victoria Hotel and a plot of land at the summit for a hotel to be built there by Assheton-Smith personally. A second agreement, made on 16 October 1894 required Cragg to transfer the land and leases to HRCNW.

By an agreement made on 16 November 1894, HRCNW was to transfer the property to SMTH in exchange for 600 fully-paid £10 SMTH shares to be issued when the property transfers had been completed. HRCNW shareholders included John Sutherland Harmood Banner, a chartered accountant from Liverpool, Rowland E. L. Naylor, Turner, Stewart, and Cragg. Its function served, HRCNW was to be wound up voluntarily in February 1896, when Banner was appointed liquidator.

The agreement between SMTH and the contractors was also made on 16 November 1894. Plans, drawings, sections and specifications had been prepared by Fox, now appointed, with his brother, the company's engineer, for the tramroad, stations 'and works necessary or incidental', also for 'the rolling stock, plant and articles necessary for the equipment and working of the said tramroad.' The contractors were required to 'construct, complete and equip' to the 'reasonable' satisfaction of the company's engineers and to the satisfaction of the Board of Trade and to 'deliver over the tramroad and works to the company fit to be opened for public traffic for passengers and goods' by 1 July 1895. The contract price was £64,000.

The contractors were to pay for any additional works or equipment required to meet the inspecting officer's requirements, even if they had not been specified. They were to start work as soon as the company had given possession of the land or not later than two months after signing the contract. They were to pay all expenses of and incidental to the company's and HRCNW's incorporation and the land

purchase. They were to take the risk that £64,000 was sufficient to complete the works as required and would be paid £64,000 in fully-paid £10 shares. While any shares remained unissued the contractors could require the company to issue a prospectus for the unissued shares on terms to be agreed by them, the net proceeds of any money received for such shares being paid to the contractors in lieu of shares.

The 'specification of works and equipment' that accompanied the contract emphasised that the latter was for 'a fixed amount without extras' and required 'the entire completion ready for public traffic of a single line of tramroad (with passing places) of the gauge 2ft 7½in.' Although not mentioned specifically in the contract, it was to be an Abt rack railway and having continental origins the gauge converts to a very precise 800mm. After opening to public traffic the contractors were to maintain the works, equipment and permanent way for three months. The company would not be liable to compensate them if there was any delay in making the land available.

Concerning the contractors' labour force, wages were to be paid in 'current coin of the realm'. The contractors were responsible for preventing riotous and unlawful conduct by their men and were to provide suitable housing for them within reasonable distance. The designs of huts or other dwellings were to be approved by the engineers who could specify 'such sanitary arrangements and precautions as they may think necessary for the health of the men … Each man shall be provided with a separate bed which shall not be occupied during his absence.'

SMTH put the onus of establishing 'the strata to be passed through, the character of the excavations, the water or snow to be expected and the nature of the soil …' on the contractors. The formation in cuttings was to be 12ft wide, on embankments 10ft wide. Three miles, presumably half that amount of route, of 'substantial dry fence walls' were to be topped with 'two seven-strand wires fixed thereon upon iron standards let into large stones with sheep netting between.' The remainder of the route was to be substantially fenced with wire netting. There were to be 14 level crossings 8ft wide with iron gates and padlocks. Gradient and mileposts 'of approved pattern' were to be provided and installed.

Station buildings at the termini and two intermediate stations were to be of 'neat but plain' design with rubble walls, slate roofs and 'well-seasoned' timber floors, doors and windows. Each was to have five rooms, including WC accommodation for men and women. Platforms of sufficient length for three cars were to be 15ft wide. The station specification was not adopted at Llanberis.

The running shed, to accommodate four locomotives and three carriages, was to be 130ft long and 40ft wide and built of stone with a slate roof. A water crane, coal stage and ashpit were to be constructed at the entrance.

A General Post Office-specification two-wire telephone system was to be installed with 'speaking and receiving instruments' at each station and both of the hotels.

In summary, the contractors were told that the 'tramroad and equipment shall be equal in detail and quality to the Brünig railway of Switzerland except where otherwise specified.' Opened between Alpnachstad and Brienze, in 1888, the 28-mile metre-gauge Brünigbahn remains a part of Swiss Federal Railways.

Compliance with the condition to satisfy the requirements of the Board of Trade, whilst well-intentioned, would be difficult to meet. As a railway built without parliamentary powers the Board of Trade had no status on it. We shall never know just how serious any of the parties were about the expectation that a mountain railway could be built in a little over seven months.

The date of the company's registration and those agreements, 16 November 1894, was also the date of the first board meeting, held in Chester. Of the promoters, Clegg, Stewart and Cragg were present. They confirmed an agreement made on 8 November to appoint themselves together with Banner, Naylor and Turner as directors. Lord Alexander Paget was also appointed a director and Turner was appointed secretary. The loan of £5,000 from the HRCNW was approved to be repaid from the proceeds of the issue of the debentures, while £2,756 was used to purchase the Victoria Hotel's furniture and effects.

With the legal structure in place, the survey to produce working plans and sections was started on 2 December 1894. An article about the line and its construction in the 3 April 1896 edition of *Engineering* says that the route as built did not match Oswell's preliminary survey at all, partly because Assheton-Smith had made objections requiring a considerable deviation to the first half of it. Other alterations were made to equalise gradients, reduce earthworks and to improve views, with the effect of taking the line 60ft closer to the summit.

All the directors were present when the board next met, on 15 December, the day of the sod-cutting ceremony. The construction contract was approved and the conveyance of the Vaynol Estate land was sealed. When the agreement with HRCNW was confirmed the directors with an interest in HRCNW abstained. Banner was appointed chairman of the board.

In 1895, Fox bound copies of documents relating to the contract together for the company's use, from which the following information has been extracted:

Projected capital expenditure

Cost of land	£1,500	
Add 5%	£75	£1,575
Earthworks		£26,200
Permanent way		£17,973
Engineering	£2,808	
Add 5%	£140	£2,948
Law and other expenses		£1,500
Compensation to farmers		£100
Hotel at summit		£6,000
Architects' commission on hotel		£300
Furnishing hotel	£1,000	
Add 5%	£50	£1,050
Water supply to hotel		£200
Refurnishing Victoria Hotel including stock and valuation	£4,000	
Add 5%	£200	£4,200
Four locomotives	£6,400	
12 carriages	£4,800	
Four trucks	£800	£12,000
Syndicate		£6,000
Electric light		£1,500
Signalling	£1,500	
Add 5%	£75	£1,575
Underwriting		£4,500
Working capital		£2,000
		£89,621

With a share capital of £70,000 the company needed to borrow up to £20,000 to fulfil its ambitions. Fox calculated that if 300 passengers paying 3s each were carried on 130 days per year the railway would earn £5,850 annually, an amount that would be increased to £11,700 if two locos were used and the passenger numbers doubled to 600 per day. The probable revenue, however, was more likely to be in the region of £8,775. The engineers calculated that two locos could operate an hourly service from Llanberis, making the return journey in two hours; they made no provision for taking fuel and water, or for cleaning the fires. Likely working expenses were calculated as shown in the table.

Estimate of working expenses

Worked with two locomotives – 130 working days	
130 days – two locomotives, including driver, cleaner, coal, oil and depreciation @ £2	£520
Two guards @ 6s	12s
Two platelayers @ 5s	10s
Four porters @ 5s	£1
130 days @ £2 8s	£312
235 non-working days @ £2 8s	£258 10s
365 days – six carriages @ 1s	£109 10s
Coal for station etc	£20
Secretary	£300
Contingencies	£50
	£1,570
Add for taxes, say 10%	£157
	£1,727

Two locomotives working five trips each per day would work 90 miles per day, 11,700 train miles over 130 days, at a cost of 2s 11½d train per mile

Estimated revenue		£8,220
Less expenses		£1,727
Balance for dividend	8½%	£6,493

Worked with four locomotives – 130 working days

130 days – four locomotives, including driver, cleaner, coal, oil and depreciation @ £2	£520
Four guards @ 6s	12s
Two platelayers @ 5s	10s
Four porters @ 5s	£1
Booking clerk @ 6s	6s
130 days @ £3	£390
235 non-working days	
One engine driver @ 6s	6s
Two platelayers @ 5s	10s
One booking clerk @ 6s	6s
235 days @ £1 2s	
365 days – six carriages @ 1s	£109 10s
Coal for station etc	£20
Secretary	£300
Contingencies	£50
	£2,270 10s
Add for taxes, say 10%	£227 10s
	£2,505

Four locomotives working five trips each per day would work 180 miles per day, 23,400 train miles over 130 days, at a cost of 2s 1½d train per mile

Estimated revenue		£8,220
Less expenses		£2,505
Balance for dividend	7½%	£5,715

Rinecker, Abt & Company provided a technical specification of the materials to be used in the rack and an exposition on the relationship between the rack and the bearing rails. These were dated 15 and 13 January 1895 respectively. Rack bars and chairs were to be steel, bolts, fishplates and couplings of wrought iron. The specification of the rack bars was particularly detailed, requiring them to be rolled with the Abt trademark and stamped with a batch number. Rinecker, Abt's inspector was to be present during manufacture and his requirements for testing were to be accommodated. Before delivery all rack components except chairs were to be cleaned and dipped in hot boiled linseed oil. The chairs were to be painted with the Maritime & General Improvement Company's black varnish. The components required to make 1,800mm of rack are shown below.

Rack bars	2
Chairs	2
Top bolts with nuts	4
Base bolts with nuts	4
Spring washers	8
Fishplates	2
Couplings of base bolts	2

Fox specified, on 19 February 1895, the bearing rail to weigh 41¼lb per yard and to be manufactured to the Indian State Railways specification. All track materials were to be stamped 'S. M. T.' and have the year and name of the manufacturer rolled into them.

There are no drawings surviving of the route as intended. The specification describes the Llanberis terminus as being near the Victoria Hotel and about 200 yards from the LNWR station. The land was a part of the hotel estate and the need for it might explain why the company acquired the hotel. No deviations from the plans were to be allowed without the engineers' approval, although the specification reveals that a deviation at Ceunant Mawr waterfalls had already been surveyed, no doubt arising from Assheton-Smith's objections. The falls have a fall of 100ft in two stages and judging by the number of picture postcards that illustrate them they were once much more popular attractions than they are now.

The *Engineering* article already referred to says that the surveyors had difficulty keeping in advance of construction. The most difficult section to lay out was a 30-chain section near Clogwyn, where the first 1-in-5½ gradient was encountered. The segment was on a continuous curve, mostly 10 chains, and the end of it had to reach a specified altitude to meet firm ground.

It is unfortunate that, apart from Abt's general specifications of the rack system, locomotives, track and turnouts, which would have been issued to any intending purchaser, no user specifications for the locomotives and rolling stock have survived, for compliance with them turned out to be an issue before too long.

Returning now to 15 December 1894 and the first sod ceremony, on that day the *Manchester Guardian* added some detail of the intended railway: it would have maximum gradients of 1 in 5½, 264ft (4 chains) maximum radius, tramcar-type carriages to accommodate at least 50 passengers with seats facing fore and aft and tilted to suit the gradient, two cars to form a train, the line would be nearly five miles long and the journey time would be less than an hour. 'To begin with, powerful steam locomotives will be employed … but eventually it is intended to adopt electricity as the chief motive power, the steam locomotives being supplementary in case of a stress of traffic… The route has been carefully chosen to afford the best view of the surrounding district during the journey, including the Ceunant Mawr waterfall, which will in no way be interfered with; and care has been taken not to spoil the appearance of the mountain itself.'

Had it been possible to use the waterfall to generate electricity then the railway might well have been electrified from the start, but no other suitable water sources were identified. A lake could have been enlarged to make a reservoir but the directors wanted to complete and open the railway as soon as possible.

The sod-cutting ceremony was a grand affair, starting with a procession led by the Llanberis Subscription brass band. Including friendly societies and tradesmen, the procession met

the Assheton-Smiths at the entrance to the village and led them to the site. The *North Wales Chronicle* estimated crowds in the order of 3,000 and some 200 invited guests. The sound of rock cannon signalled the start of proceedings. Introduced by Sir Douglas Fox, Assheton-Smith gave his daughter, nine-year-old Enid, a miniature spade with which she dug and placed the first sod into a miniature wheelbarrow. These tools, there was a pickaxe as well, were decorated with sterling silver and gold, and were mounted on an ebony base which had a silver shield engraved 'First sod of the Snowdon Tramroad cut 15th December, by Miss Assheton-Smith'. Assheton-Smith's wife, Laura Alice, was to have performed the ceremony but was ill. The tools are now in private ownership; it has not been possible to establish their whereabouts.

Amongst the speeches delivered before the guests adjourned for lunch, Assheton-Smith made what must have been an unexpected comment about 'the hotel keepers and others who catered for … visitors.' If the railway brought the tourists back to Llanberis he hoped that they 'would not make the mistake of imposing extortionate charges and so drive people away again', saying that Llanberis had a reputation for extortionate charges and unsatisfactory accommodation.

Lunch, prepared by a Liverpool caterer and served at the Victoria Hotel, was followed by more speeches. Assheton-Smith took the opportunity to comment on the dispute with Rawnsley. Saying that it was true that he, Assheton-Smith, had changed his mind about the Snowdon railway he had heard that Rawnsley was also a man who changed his mind. He, Rawnsley, had apparently objected to Manchester Corporation's plan for a reservoir in Thirlmere yet had been one of the first to congratulate the corporation when it was completed.

The *Manchester Guardian's* reporter included in his account the information that the summit hotel would be located on a half-acre site, have thick stone walls to protect it from the elements, and have 25 beds.

The symbolic start of construction did not bring an end to criticism of the project, for on 26 December the *Manchester Guardian's* Welsh correspondent commented on the first sod ceremony and complained that the 'promoters of the enterprise have chosen to figure as the friends of humanity, inspired by a consuming anxiety to benefit the weak and infirm …' before continuing 'what has afforded many not a little amusement has been the spectacle of several estimable Welsh public men posing as philanthropists in this carnival of unmitigated Philistinism.' After targeting the Bishop of Bangor he went on 'but the two most facetious statements of the day were made by Mr D. P. Williams and Sir Douglas Fox, the engineer. Mr Williams expressed his opinion that "the railway would mark an era in the history of Wales." There are few gentlemen who are usually more measured and sober in their utterances than the respected ex-chairman of the Carnarvonshire County Council, and one scarcely expected that the [railway] would have led him to lose so grievously his sense of proportion. Sir Douglas Fox, however, eclipsed both the bishop and Mr Williams when he declared that "every care has been taken to deal in the most tender way with all the beautiful scenery."'

The *North Wales Chronicle* had, incidentally, reported that SMTH's motto was *'sic itur ad astra'*, a quote from Virgil's *Aeneid*, 'thus you shall go to the stars'. The newspaper thought it was rather a joke and, joke or not, that seems to have been the first and last time that it was mentioned. Within 18 months the company's star had fallen to the ground with a resounding crash.

2

Construction and inspection

Despite the letting of the construction contract and the first sod having been cut, there was still a great deal of work to be done before trains could be run. Amongst the business carried out by the board on 29 January 1895 was the allotment of £6,000 of shares to HRCNW. It also resolved to invite applications for the post of manager and secretary.

Shares were issued, one each, to the signatories of the company's articles, on 16 February. On the same date, transfers from HRCNW in favour of Holme, George Nicholson, J. W. Heblethwaite, Stewart, Naylor, Banner, J. Marke Wood, John Ernest Greaves, Cecil W. Cragg, Wallace W. Cragg and Turner were approved. Heblethwaite and Naylor had 75 shares each, the rest 50 each. John Ernest Greaves was the owner of the Llechwedd slate quarry at Blaenau Ffestiniog; his shares were to be transferred to Edward Seymour Greaves on 31 May.

Following a decision to issue £35,000 of first mortgage debentures the board resolved to accept the offer by the company's bankers, Leyland & Bullins, Liverpool, to cash a £1,500 4% debenture payable on 31 July 1895. Presumably the purpose of this arrangement was to provide the company with working capital.

Details of the early works are sparse. Fox had submitted a letter reporting progress to the 16 February meeting and on 28 March the board resolved to inform him that he was not to authorise any extras without the directors' approval. His attempts to obtain payment were rebuffed by the directors in March and May; on the second occasion they offered half of the £600 requested, to be paid after shares had been allotted.

The first rails were delivered on 27 March via Carnarvon, arriving thence on board the steamship *Solway King*, an iron vessel built on the Ribble in 1883. Unloading took 50 hours instead of the scheduled 24 owing to the lack of labour to clear the wharf. The ship's owners sued the contractors for 7s 6d an hour demurrage, £9 15s. In court in May, the contractors' barrister successfully argued that the contract was with the consignors, Richard White & Son, iron merchants of Widnes, not the consignees. The judge agreed and at the resumed hearing in June, when the consignors were heard, the judge ruled that the delay had not been as much as claimed and awarded £5 5s to the plaintiffs.

Three candidates for the post of secretary and manager had appeared before the board on 10 April 1895 and Gowrie Colquhoun Aitchison was appointed on a two-year contract that could be terminated by the directors at three months' notice. His salary was to be £300, without a house, for the first year and he was to be responsible for the working the tramroad, hotels and refreshment rooms, to make all returns, keep accounts, conduct correspondence and 'generally organise traffic.' Born in 1863 in Poona, India, Aitchison had been educated at Clifton College, Bristol, and Queen's College, Cambridge. He had previously worked as an assistant farm manager and had married into a family of land agents at South Collingham, Lincolnshire, which in due course was to influence the end of his railway career.

Following board approval on 9 May, the prospectus for £20,000 in £100 4½% debentures and 6,343 £10 shares was issued on 21 May 1895. It stated that the share capital was to fund the railway's construction whilst the debentures, to be redeemable at par after 10 years, were to fund the hotels, land required and other expenses not included in the construction contract. Half of the formation had been constructed and partially ballasted and it

A Fox-produced plan of the railway, 1896, with the intermediate loops identified as turnouts. The railway and lakes have been highlighted. *Author's collection*

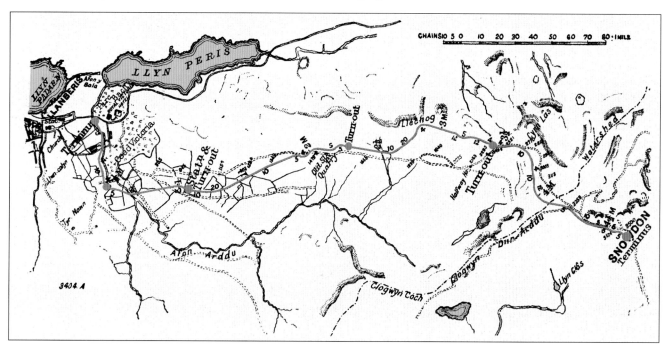

was anticipated that the tramroad could be completed and ready for passenger traffic 'during the present season'.

The Victoria Hotel estate comprised the hotel and 32 acres of land, including Dolbadarn Castle, and fishing rights. Estimating that profits should not be less than 8% of capital, the directors likened the undertaking to the Swiss Rigibahn and noted that that line had been paying 8% on £50,000 capital after paying interest on £38,000 debentures and without any hotel revenue. By 31 May, the company had received 13 applications for shares and ten for debentures.

Writing on 17 May, Fox had informed the directors that the report was included in the prospectus, the centre line had been set out and levelled for 3½ miles from Llanberis, and earthworks were in progress over three miles; 1¾ miles was ready for track and ½ mile ready for bottom ballast. Good progress had been made with the abutments and piers of the lower viaduct and those for the upper viaduct were nearly ready for the arches to be formed. Four bridges were ready for concreting.

Stone was being used for the piers and abutments of the viaducts, culverts and bridges, and brick arches adopted where possible. Ornamental timber would be used for the Llanberis station building, while the other stations would be 'simple buildings, of local stone'. A locomotive and carriage shed would be provided to house and repair the rolling stock. There would be four locomotives and three trains of two carriages, each train accommodating 112 passengers.

The Societé Suisse pour la Construction de Locomotives et de Machines (in German Schweizerische Locomotiv & Maschinenfabrik, ie, the Swiss Locomotive Company – SLM) had despatched the first locomotive from its Winterthur works via Antwerp on 10 June 1895. J. H. Welsford & Company invoiced the contractors £46 15s 11d for the charges incurred in dealing with the import of No 1 received from the SS *Ptarmigan*. Unloading the loco took 54 man-hours at 6d per hour. The LNWR charged £14 15s 9d for the delivery to Llanberis. No 2 arrived at Llanberis on 3 August. The 10 August report in the *North Wales Chronicle* describes how it was transported between the LNWR station and the SMR using temporary rails laid along the road, a method that was presumably used for the other rolling stock. The locomotives cost £1,525 each, inclusive of the Abt royalty.

The contractors appeared to be confident about progress, for on 9 July 1895 they proposed that as soon as the railway was finished they would operate it until the end of the season at their own expense. They would use the company's locomotives and carriages and take the revenue. In return for this they would pay the shareholders 5% interest on the issued share capital 'as soon as possible after 1 January next.' The offer was accepted by the board the next day. At the same time approval was given to the loco shed being built of timber with stone foundation and slate roof instead of the rubble walls specified in the contract.

The contractors' offer was probably designed to distract the directors, because the Cardiff-based *Western Mail* had already, on 27 May, forecast that the railway was not likely to be ready. According to the paper, the track was already at Halfway but the work had progressed more slowly than anticipated. The account of No 2's delivery forecast an opening at the end of September.

Fox told the directors that he had certified work valued £25,044 on 10 July 1895 and they issued 2,100 shares in part

payment. When the shares were re-allocated on 25 September, the contractors kept 743 for the partnership, 286 for Holme and his wife and 236 for King and his daughter, effectively putting Holme in control of the company. On 21 June, the contractors had submitted a statement of their current position and a breakdown of the track materials already obtained.

Earthworks	Contract total	£26,200	
	Still to do	£8,664	£17,536
Permanent way	Materials on ground		£4,929
			£22,465
		Less 10%	£2,246
			£20,219
Provisions	Law and other expenses		£750
	Locos on account		£1,500
	Advertising		£1,152
	Underwriting		£2,000
			£25,621

23 March	307 tons 18cwt 2qtr – rails	£7 per ton	£2,155 9s 6d
	37 tons 16cwt 3qtr – fishplates	£10 per ton	£378 7s 6d
11 April/10 May	47,300 Grover spring washers	£4 per 1,000	£188 14s
2 May	7,200 fish bolts, 2 tons, 12cwt, 1qtr 4lb	£12 10s per ton	£32 17s
1 June	2,000 yard – rack rail with fastenings	£1,760 per mile	£2,000
7 June	5½ steel sleepers	£7 10s per ton	£41 5s
19 June	3,300 fish bolts, 1 ton 3qtr 7lb	£12 10s per ton	£13
20 June	3 tons – rail clips and bolts	£40 per ton	£120
			£4,929 13s

Components for the rack had been supplied by Charles Cammell & Company Ltd of Sheffield; a delivery note for components to make up two miles was dated 29 June 1895. They had been despatched via the Manchester, Sheffield & Lincolnshire Railway in four wagons, Nos 15524, 5588, 213 and 13100. Bolts supplied by White from Widnes had been despatched on the same date. According to the contemporary technical press White was the main sub-contractor for the track materials. Whilst Cammell rolled the bars at its Sheffield plant, it was the Yorkshire Engine Company that cut the teeth into them. Fishplates were made at Cammell's Workington plant and sleepers by the Ebbw Vale Steel, Iron & Coal Ltd. In 1899 Yorkshire Engine had surplus rack bars in stock and Aitchison was to be authorised to offer scrap price for them.

The Lancaster Carriage & Wagon Company demonstrated its progress with the carriages by submitting doors for inspection on 10 July. The board approved and instructed that they be painted in the colours shown.

Aitchison was well entrenched in his position by 6 August, for the board instructed him to 'visit the Swiss mountain railways' as soon as possible. What he learned during his 28-day visit was not recorded. Fox had, incidentally, made a three-week tour of European rack railways in November 1894 and his 16-page hand-written report is contained in the specification volume.

In anticipation of opening, Aitchison was instructed to recruit a stationmaster and superintendent and fares were set at: return - 5s maximum/4s minimum; up – 3s 6d/2s 6d; down 2s 6d/2s. G. W. North was subsequently appointed, the post was not specified, at £1 5s per week with effect from 1 January 1896; Aitchison was given authority to increase the rate of pay when the railway started operating.

The board appeared to be unhappy with Fox and work carried out by the contractors when it met on 13 November, resolving to refer the size of the engine and carriage shed to him and asking if he had authorised it. Aitchison was told to inform Fox that the directors wished to be consulted about any plans before the work was undertaken. Fox was also to be informed that if there were any savings made on any work he should ensure that they were credited to the company.

Having received three locomotives the directors decided, also on 13 November, to order a fourth and to get prices from English builders to compare with SLM. On 7 December Aitchison was instructed to request Fox to order the locomotive and two more carriages, delivery to be before the end of May 1896. It is not clear if the 7 December instruction was for a fifth locomotive or merely a repeat of the earlier decision.

By the time of a report published in the *North Wales Chronicle* on 30 November, work had been sufficiently advanced for Oswell, now Fox's resident engineer, to issue permits for 'trial trips'. Track had been laid within ¾ mile of the summit, workmen were working on the 'steepest and most dangerous portion' of the railway and, although the 'nipping cold and short days' prevented much work from being carried out, track laying would be completed within a few weeks. This was despite the *Liverpool Mercury* having already, on 12 November, announced the suspension of work due to severe weather.

By the end of the year, Fox had issued five construction certificates. No 3, approved on 30 October was for £12,218; the contractors were paid £14,872 by cheque and £1,390 in fully-paid shares. On the figures given SMTH had overpaid by £10 at this stage. The company's bankers were asked to loan the company £14,172 at 4% against future income on its share allotment and first-call accounts. Fox was paid £750 on account of his commission. Certificates Nos 4 and 5 were issued on 7 December 1895, for £5,070 and a cheque was issued for the full amount. There is no indication available about how much of this

Top: **The cutting below Halfway, ready for track laying. At about 20ft, it is the deepest on the line.** *Clinton Holme/ Author's collection*

Above: **A smaller cutting near the summit awaits the arrival of the track gang.** *Clinton Holme/Author's collection*

Right: **Another view nearby, the discarded tools on the left serving as a reminder of the primitive equipment available to the contractors.** *Beecham/Author's collection*

money was for construction and how much was for equipment, but expenditure of some £43,000 compared to the construction and equipment budget of £64,000 suggests that there was still a good proportion of work to be carried out.

No explanation for the contractors' failure to meet the 1 July completion date has been uncovered. They must have thought the railway was nearly finished when they offered to run it until the end of the season. It is speculative to draw attention to the unexplained resignations of Stewart and Lord Alexander Paget from the board during the autumn – maybe they were unhappy at the apparently slow progress. In Stewart's case there could well have been a conflict of interest with his position as Assheton-Smith's agent.

There were 10 gangs of 10 to 25 men according to *Engineering*. Hourly rates varied according to the height being worked at: labourers, 5d/6½d; masons, 8½d/10½d. They lived in huts erected by the contractors, one at each 'halfway house', and stayed there from Sunday evening until Saturday. The contractors supplied soup every day when it was cold. Iron-shod sleighs hauled by three horses carried materials up the mountain before the rails were laid. It took half a day to drag 7cwt to the second halfway house, a distance of three miles. To maintain continuity of access during construction temporary bridges were erected on the sites of the bridges crossing the bridle path below Hebron and above Clogwyn.

Engineering explained that experience had shown that the best results were obtained by laying the sleepers and the rack before the rails. The 4mm play in positioning the rack was tested by using a stepping gauge across four teeth in the adjacent bars before they were tightened up. On the inside of curves the rails were shorter than on the outside; there were five combinations for the five radii used. On 2 September, 14 men started tracklaying above the viaducts, finishing on 6 January 1896 – 72 working days. The average length laid per day was 122 yards; the best day's work was 350 yards, and the best week, nearly 1,500 yards. Track on the section below the viaducts had been laid before 2 September.

The *Railway Times* published on 18 January 1896 reported that a train comprising a locomotive and two carriages, and carrying 'a few passengers connected with the project' had reached the summit on 10 January. The magazine, which said that the line was completed except for fencing and signalling, concluded its report: 'The line will not be opened to the public at present, but several trains will run, it is thought, to accommodate the Easter excursion traffic.'

There was no mention of that first trip to the summit when the board met on 16 January 1896, but Fox was asked to arrange for a Board of Trade inspection. Construction certificates Nos 6 and 7 were mentioned but their value was not recorded; payment would be made when the contractors had met the calls on their shares which were in arrears; a balance cheque for £6,543 was to be issued to the contractors on 12 February. Regarding the boundaries, the board agreed to the walling above the river bridge being replaced by fencing subject to Assheton-Smith agreeing. Neither of the English companies that had quoted to supply a locomotive could deliver before August and SLM, which had quoted £1,575, could not guarantee delivery before the end of July. Holme agreed to the company dealing with SLM direct, using the equipment budget, and waived his claim for commission on the order.

Fox gave the board a report on an accident involving 'No 2 engine' when it met on 12 February 1896, but no other details were recorded; a report into the 6 April accident was to give a date of 31 January for this one. It was subsequently reported that it had become the practice to run trains carrying workmen up and down the line and that there were several occasions when the loco mounted the rack during the construction; no importance was attached to these incidents, presumably, it was suggested, because the works were unfinished.

Newly arrived from Switzerland, the ill-fated No 1 *L. A. D. A. S.* was used during construction. The occasion of the photograph is not known but the group appears to include more management than labourers. The driver is probably Pickles. *SMR*

Left: **Out on the big viaduct, a locomotive was photographed with one of the wagons.** *L. C. Symons/SMR*

Below: **Surveying just above the second viaduct during construction.** *Clinton Holme/Author's collection*

The company's negotiations with SLM had borne fruit to the extent that two locomotives were ordered – perhaps the builder was prepared to give a better delivery, and price, for two. In March it was to be agreed that the cost of locomotive spares and 'two more carriages' should be taken from the £12,000 equipment budget, even if ordered by the company direct.

The summit hotel was a regular item on the board's agenda and was anything but straightforward. Although Assheton-Smith had given the hut keepers six months' notice to quit on 12 May 1894, it was reported on 31 May 1895 that they refused to give up possession. Legal action was started against them in July 1895.

The board appeared to have doubts about the hotel, asking the architect, also in July 1895, to reduce the number of rooms to 17, and to include a drying room. Then on 1 October it learned that the company's application for a provisional licence had been refused and asked if Assheton-Smith was willing to forego the requirement to spend £5,000 on it; the latter might not have been consequential on the former. No answer was recorded, but in February 1896 the directors were informed that Assheton-Smith was going to install his own refreshment room at the summit. On 10 March 1895, Stewart said that, starting on 22 March, he was going to build a wall 'a few inches above the ground level' along Assheton-Smith's boundary and in front of 'Owen's hut',

Right: **Fixing the rack into position in advance of the running rails with a loco not far behind. The Dinorwic quarry complex is visible behind, with the separate Vivian quarry to the left.**
Clinton Holme/Author's collection

Below: **Newly laid track just above Waterfall. Several of the sleeper ends are not fully supported.**
Clinton Holme/Author's collection

As the line approached completion so did the fund-raising. The position at 30 November 1895 was that 6,111 £10 shares had been issued, of which £12,954 had not been called and £5,575 was in arrears; £18,200 debentures had been subscribed, of which £11,050 was uncalled. In addition to the 600 shares allocated to HRCNW to purchase the land, £39,422 had been spent on construction, engineering charges, land purchase and legal expenses.

On 30 October 1895, Aitchison had also been instructed to collect payment in full on the six, out of seven, subscriber shares that had not been paid for; perhaps their recipients thought they were a gift. By January 1896, two shareholders were in arrears with their calls and the company placed the matter

the wall being designed to accommodate the proposed building. The board decided to arrange for building a portion of the hotel's foundation to enable the platform to be completed. At the same time Owen had renewed his previously unrecorded offer to SMHT, his summit hut and its licence for £3,000; it was refused, the price being considered prohibitive.

Dealings with Assheton-Smith were handled, usually via Stewart, with kid gloves. He was the landowner, he was wealthy, he had ultimate control. The prospect of his setting up in competition for summit revenues would have horrified the directors for they must have known that a trading monopoly on the summit would be as profitable as running trains. Earlier, the board had sought to establish his position if additional land was required for a second track; he said that the company could have the option of purchasing land for doubling the line at any time at the same price per acre as the land already taken.

At Llanberis, the situation regarding public facilities was more easily dealt with. The plans were approved on 10 July 1895, after they had been altered to incorporate Aitchison's requirements, to give extra WC accommodation for both sexes, a manager's room and an office. Owen Morris's tender of £595 for its erection was accepted on 11 December.

with its solicitor. The final calls on the shares were made on 12 February, by which time one of the errant shareholders had paid up. To give the shares credence, an application for listing on the Liverpool Stock Exchange had been made in October 1895.

To promote the railway, an unsolicited offer to supply a manuscript guide to the line was accepted and Aitchison was to arrange printing in October 1895; whether this was done is not known. A meeting held with the LNWR at Euston in December resulted in an agreement to advertise in the LNWR's North Wales guide if the price was agreeable. Others saw the railway as an opportunity and in February 1896 W. H. Smith's tender for advertising at stations for three years was accepted.

The company's first annual report, published on 9 March 1896, gives a small insight into the state of construction just before the railway was due to carry its first fare-paying passengers. 'The work of constructing the tramroad has progressed satisfactorily towards completion, although it has taken considerably longer to carry out than originally expected', Banner and Aitchison wrote in the directors' report. They also noted that three locomotives and six carriages, 'being three complete trains', had been delivered. Fox's report is more

revealing and was written on 28 February, the day after another trip to the summit according to the *Railway Times*. 'The viaducts and bridges are nearly completed, as also the fence walling,' said Fox, 'the ballast is now in a forward state, and the signalling is nearly ready for work. There are several minor works, including drainage, yet to be completed, and the mountain stations have not yet been commenced. We do not see any reason why passenger traffic should not be run at Easter and we have given first notice to the Board of Trade with this view.'

When the board met on 18 March, Fox advised it to get a letter from the contractors making it clear that if the company did run trains at Easter the line was not to be considered as complete.

Fox's first notice to the Board of Trade had been submitted on 1 May 1895. Whilst one officer was prepared to find a way to permit an inspection, another noted that the president had objected to the railway (p12) and he was also opposed to voluntary inspections. Fox was seen on 20 May and a file note records that he was told the position and had agreed to inform the SMTH directors. 'It is fully clear that he is anxious that the line should be inspected to relieve himself from responsibility.'

It appears that the company did consider applying for Parliamentary powers; a letter from the solicitor on the subject was mentioned in the minutes in October 1895. At this stage, with the railway partially constructed, an application would be a high-risk and expensive strategy. Not only would it have given Rawnsley and others a fresh opportunity to object, but it might have failed.

Fox's second request to the Board of Trade for an inspection was made on 21 January 1896, when one of the officers minuted: 'I am still of opinion that we should not impose on the inspecting officers the responsibility of inspecting and approving a speculative and technical undertaking of this character. No Parliamentary powers have been obtained.

'The argument the other way is this. The directors ask for a government inspection. It is refused. There is an accident subsequently and the public will not understand why we did not use the opportunity given us to do what we could to insure public safety.'

This paragraph turned out to be prophetic. Another officer said that he would like to send Major Marindin. On 16 March, Fox caught the Board of Trade out by serving a second notice on

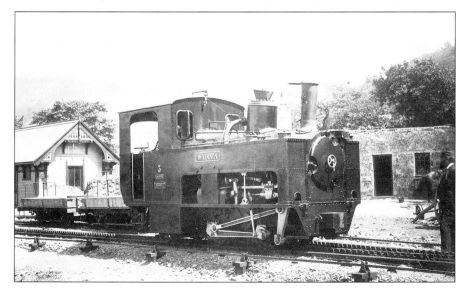

Top: **Llanberis station site before the opening, showing the station building and its relationship with the Victoria Hotel behind it. The stone building at the right now houses the railway's offices.** *Clinton Holme/Author's collection*

Left: **No 3 was probably newly delivered when photographed with two wagons at Llanberis. A short time afterwards a signal was erected that would have been visible in this view, between the loco's cab and station building. The wagons are lettered SMT&H Co Ld; the left-hand one is No 2.** *Photochrom/Author's collection*

23

Chainage M Ch	Height above sea level	Intervals	Rise in feet	Rate of rise (mean)	Comment
0·00	352.06				Water, main siding, three running shed sidings
1·07	924.72	87ch	572.66	1:10	Water, main siding, dead end siding (goods)
2·00	1,635.79	93ch	711.07	1:8.6	Water, main siding
3·30	2,526.29	90ch	890.50	1:6.7	Water, main siding
4·53	3,490.55	103ch	964.26	1:7.0	No water, main siding (dead end)

the prescribed form which cited the section 4 of the 1842 Regulation of Railways Act, 'That no railway ... shall be opened for the public conveyance of passengers ... after notice in writing of the intention of opening the same shall have been given... The promoters ... have given notice of their intention to open their line under an act ... which appears to leave the Board of Trade no option in the circumstances but to inspect it in the interests of public safety.' Major Francis A. Marindin received his orders.

Before moving on to Marindin's report, a few words about the technical description that accompanied Fox's notice are required. Compiled by Oswell on 13 March, it covers much the same ground as Aitchison's 1899 description (Appendix 1), but there are some additional items. Facilities along the line were given in the table (*above*).

There are 35 curves along the route, he said, their aggregate length amounting to 42½% of the whole, the radii being 3.90, 4, 5, 10, 12 and 20 chains. Eight bridges and viaducts were as listed in the table (*below*).

The last, intended to carry the bridle path over the railway was not built. There were also six culverts with spans ranging from 3ft to 6ft. The first bridge, by the end of the loco shed, had no handrails.

The carriages were 38ft long overall, 6ft 6in wide and 9ft 4in high. They weighed 5 tons 13cwt empty, about 9 tons laden, and had seven eight-seat compartments with a coupé at the front for the guard. The latter operated the brake which was connected to a double pinion carried on its own axle mounted in the centre of the down-hill bogie frame. The bogie centres were 28ft apart and the carriages were unglazed with canvas curtains provided to keep out the weather. The length of a complete train was 91ft.

Marindin's report was submitted on 3 April, Good Friday; his inspection had taken place on 27 March. A detailed description of the railway, presumably supplied by Fox, which is very fulsome, was published in *Engineering* in instalments from 3 April and contains details of the inspection not mentioned by Marindin. His

Structure	Chainage M Ch	Type	Material	Span	Crossing	Height
Bridge	0 7½	Girder	Steel	30ft	Stream	
Viaduct	0 15	Viaduct	Masonry, 14 30ft semi-circular brick arches	500ft		43ft
Viaduct	0 32	Viaduct	Masonry, 4 30ft semi-circular brick arches	190ft		37ft
Bridge	0 53	Masonry	Brick segmental arch	50ft	Stream	10ft
Bridge	0 75	Masonry	Brick semi-arch	15ft	Occupation road	
Bridge	2 0	Concrete/girders			Bridle path	
Bridge	3 40	Concrete/girders			Bridle path	
Bridge	4 18	Girder	Light steel		Tramroad	

Right: **Just above the upper viaduct with Waterfall station in the centre distance Compare with the construction view of the location on p22.** *Author's collection*

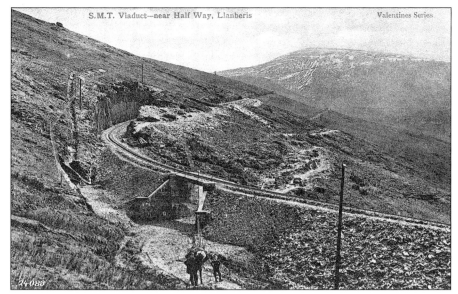

S.M.T. Viaduct—near Half Way, Llanberis   Valentines Series

Left: **Below Halfway, showing the bridge over the bridle path.** *Valentine/ Author's collection*

Below: **Looking downhill at the reverse curves at the same location.** *Author's collection*

Bottom: **Gradient profile**

train, two carriages was implied, was loaded with cement to represent the passenger load. On the descent the locomotive's automatic brake was allowed 'to run full speed on a 1-in-6 gradient, and when 5mph was attained the brake automatically stopped the locomotive.' The carriages were allowed to 'run downhill separately and stopped on their own handbrakes.'

The line was 4m 53.75ch long, wrote Marindin. Of the passing places, at Hebron, Halfway and Clogwyn, only the first had a building. Waterfall had a building but no loop. For most of its length the railway was a surface line but there were a number of small embankments and cuttings, some of the latter through rock. The biggest embankment was 12.25ch long and 13.76ft high; two other embankments were 16.50ft and 16.20ft high. The biggest cutting was 34.15ch long and 16.79ft deep, the others were 14.90ch long/10.68ft deep and 9.10ch long/20.15ft deep. The only works of any large dimensions were, he said, the viaducts. 'These works have been well constructed and appear to be quite sound. The girders of the underbridges have sufficient strength and were satisfactorily tested. The brakes on the train are thoroughly efficient, the train being under perfect control, both on the ascending and descending journey, and when detached from the engine each carriage can be stopped, or let down slowly as may be desired, on the steepest gradients, by means of the brake attached to it.'

He thought that it would be 'desirable to devise some method of preventing a driver from tampering in any way with the automatic brake, which, when set to come into action when the regulated speed is exceeded, should not be ... to be altered at the discretion of the driver.'

Semaphore signals were worked from ground frames at Llanberis (six levers), Hebron (seven), Halfway (six), Clogwyn (six) and Summit (four). The points at Waterfall were locked by the train staff. The slow speed and ability to stop trains very quickly rendered distant signals unnecessary, Marindin said. He thought that disc signals indicating the position of points would have been sufficient for the same reason.

Concerning the fencing, he said: 'as there are only a few mountain sheep on the high ground I see no objection to the proposal to dispense with fences above 2m 70ch provided a grid is placed across the line at the termination of the fencing.'

There was still a good deal of work to be done on the station buildings but he did not think that that should hinder the line being opened. He did require, however, a 'substantial' buffer stop at the end of the platform line at the summit. At Hebron he

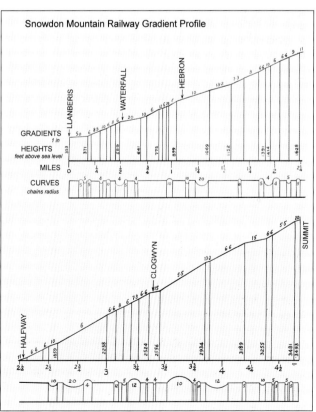

25

thought that a second platform should be provided. Concerning the trains, he thought that life guards fitted to the leading ends of the carriages would be a benefit.

Marindin foresaw that high winds would render the carriages 'liable to upset' and listed six combinations, ranging from trains being full to empty and with the curtains being open or half closed, that would cause concern at different wind speeds. He identified the line above Clogwyn as a location of particular concern and recommended that one or more wind gauges should be erected and train operation suspended 'whenever a dangerous pressure is recorded'.

The Board of Trade sent a copy of the report to the company on 4 April, the draft covering letter being altered to make Marindin's recommendations advisory instead of mandatory. The board had instructed Aitchison to buy a wind gauge on 18 March.

Amongst the pre-opening visitors was a party of engineers from the LNWR, the Midland Railway and the Manchester, Sheffield & Lincolnshire Railway who travelled on the 24 March, leaving Llanberis at 10pm. The group included F. W. Webb, the LNWR's locomotive engineer, and Sir Edward Leader Williams, the Manchester Ship Canal's engineer.

Local residents paid reduced fares to travel on a special train on 4 April. A large stone rolled out of a cutting near to the summit and derailed the leading carriage bogie of their train; Aitchison was to tell the inquest that this happened two or three minutes from the summit, but it could have been at or very close to the site where the accident was to occur on 6 April.

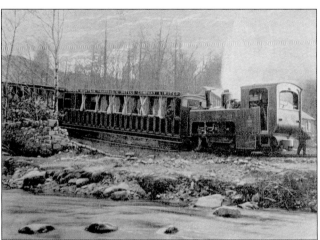

Top: **Near the summit and showing the rack without the angle irons. The first station building has been built, the telegraph installed and the signals erected. The boards in the foreground imply that the track gang is not far away.** *Photochrom/Author's collection*

Middle: **A test train at the foot of the lower viaduct.** *Clinton Holme/ Author's collection*

Below: **This well-known photograph shows how the SMR was intended to be, with two carriages propelled by the locomotive. It was obviously posed and may show one of the pre-opening trial workings.** *LNWR/Author's collection*

SNOWDON MOUNTAIN RAILWAY TRAIN
VIA LLANBERIS STATION. L.& N.W. RAILWAY.

Above: **Another posed photograph shows two carriages with No 2** *Enid* **apparently painted black and with a Continental-style lamp.** *L. C. Symons/Valentine/Author's collection*

Below: **Gowrie Colquhoun Aitchison (front, centre) with his staff. His chair still exists and is kept in the manager's office.** *SMR*

3

The first day and its aftermath

In preparation for the opening, the *Manchester Guardian* published an article about the railway on 4 April 1896. The Snowdon Mountain Railway was, it said, outclassed by the Swiss Pilatus line and would seem a small thing beside the daring Jungfraubahn in the Bernese Oberland. It was, nevertheless, a work of magnitude and originality, an entirely new step in British railway enterprise. It was designed to incorporate the best of these lines, not to copy any one of them. It was, however, an experiment pure and simple and its failure or success would determine whether a system that flourished in Switzerland was capable of success in Britain.

A trial trip operated for the press earlier in the week had been accompanied by Aitchison, Oswell and Rigby, the contractors' foreman. 'Looking back on the journey', wrote the journalist, 'one is struck by the entire absence of anything that could make it sensational. The ascent is safe, gradual, uneventful. There are no dangerous-looking stages to attract the adventurous and to frighten the timid – no chasms crossed by slender bridges, no overhanging crags that threaten to crush you. It is all plain sailing… It is, as already intimated, a pure experiment, but when it has become better known and the dread of a possible accident has passed away it is expected to attract a sufficient stream of tourists into the district to reward the enterprise and outlay of the promoters …' The suggestion that a new venture might be accompanied by danger is clearly not a recent one. (A much shorter report published in the *Times* on 6 April, which included the same comment about the railway being an experiment, said that there had been several trial trips.)

On 6 April, Easter Monday, the weather started fine. A pilot train was run to the summit and left personnel at their stations as it returned. Without ceremony, No 1 *L. A. D. A. S.* propelled the first public train of two carriages, conveying 83 passengers, up the mountain at 10.50am, later than intended because the LNWR connection was late. A second train of a single carriage propelled by No 2 *Enid* left some 20 minutes later. The first train started its return journey to Llanberis just after 12.30pm.

Reaching a point 100yd above the bridge crossing the Llanberis path, the automatic brake activated, indicating that the train speed had exceeded 5½-6mph. After the brake was reset, the journey resumed, Aitchison telling the driver to go slowly. Restarting, the driver, William Pickles, was to say that the loco lurched to one side; telling the fireman to jump off, he applied the brakes and, as the loco's speed increased, jumped off himself. On the train, Aitchison and Oswell, one in each carriage, applied the brakes, bringing it to a stand, within 30yd Aitchison was to say. Two men ignored his shouted order to remain seated and jumped off, one of them falling as he did so and breaking his leg.

The locomotive meanwhile, having completely derailed, continued downhill, hitting a telegraph pole and literally flying

Fox's plan showing the scene of the accident was produced for the inquest into the death of Ellis Griffith Roberts. *National Archives*

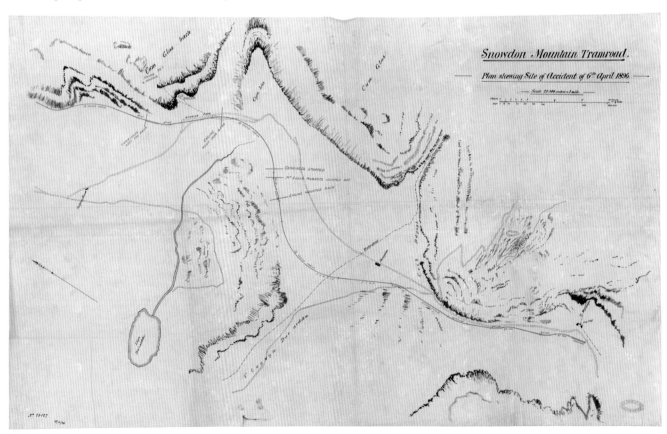

over the Llanberis path, missing several walkers, and fell several hundred feet down Cwm Glas. The breaking telegraph wires short-circuited, causing the bell to ring at the summit, a sign the crew there took as a signal to start.

By now the upper reaches of the mountain were engulfed in cloud. Aitchison sent men in each direction to protect the engine-less train but was too late to prevent the second train from colliding with the carriages of the first. Although this loco also mounted the rack, the impact made its pinion re-engage with it and it stopped. Fortunately, the first train's carriages had been evacuated, for the collision sent them off towards Clogwyn. There, the quick-thinking pointsman set the points midway, derailing the carriages; they came to a stand at the downhill end of the station without causing further injury. One of them had the coupé end stoved in where it had been hit.

The passengers from both trains were directed to continue their journey on foot and a doctor was sent for to treat the injured passenger, Ellis Griffith Roberts. Another passenger, Benjamin Blower of Shrewsbury, gave him brandy and first aid, staunching the flow of blood. Blower was not a member of an 'ambulance class' but his wife and her friend were and they told him what to do. A carriage seat was broken off and used as a make-shift stretcher. The Dinorwic quarry doctor arrived nearly three hours after the incident and supervised Roberts' removal to his home, the Padarn Villa Hotel, now using the Clogwyn cabin door as a stretcher and taking another three hours. There, Roberts's leg was amputated but he had probably lost too much blood for he died in the early hours of the following day.

Aitchison's report of the accident and the fatality, submitted to the Board of Trade on April 7, generated a flurry of

telegrams; there would be no inquiry and Marindin could attend the inquest voluntarily, at the coroner's request, to provide technical assistance. He reached Llanberis on 8 April, in time to walk up to the incident site, to return via the site of the destroyed locomotive, attend the inquest and write an informal report to a Board of Trade colleague that was posted the same day. No 1's boiler was some 250ft below the point where the loco left the line and the remainder was 250ft further down, 1,500ft above the Llanberis Pass.

At the accident site the path of the loco from the point where it became separated from the rack to the point where it went over the edge, about ¼ mile, could be clearly seen. 'The pinions,' he said, 'seem to have mounted the rack, and to have run along the top of the rack for nearly the whole distance, the carrying wheels keeping on the rails in an extraordinary way until shortly before the final leap, when the speed must have been very high.'

He could confirm that the overspeed brake had activated because the pinions were still locked when he examined them. Four of the pinion cogs had been cut out nearly an inch deep by the rack's cogs, 'as if by a chisel'. The other pinion cogs were unmarked, demonstrating the brake's grip on the axle.

He could not account for the pinion mounting the rack and speculated that 'the road at the point where this occurred had got a little rotten on the break up of the sharp touch of frost that prevailed at the time I went over the line; and that the engine must have given a bad lurch when on a sleeper which gave under the weight, but this ought not to have been sufficient to cause such a serious accident.'

'The road at that point,' he explained, 'is certainly not as solid as it was when I went over the line, but it was gauged last Thursday and thoroughly examined on Monday, and an engine and wagon were sent up and down again on Monday morning before the regular train was allowed to start.' Commenting that the efficiency of the carriage brake had been demonstrated he went on to say that some means should be found to prevent the pinion mounting the rack and that 'some additional retarding power should be provided to come into action in case the three existing brakes are rendered useless...'

The inquest was opened on 8 April. Before starting, the coroner and jury discussed, in Welsh, whether the inquest should be conducted in that language or in English. One of the jurors said that some of the jury was not fully conversant in English and there had been cases where a decision had been reached only for some jurors to admit that they had not understood all the evidence. The coroner explained that he was required to conduct the inquest in English and that if any of the jurors did not understand what was being said they were to ask.

The coroner continued that he had asked the Board of Trade for assistance and had been informed that despite the railway being built without statutory powers it would treat the situation as a special case. After taking identification evidence, the inquest was adjourned until the following week.

Resumed on 14 April at the Prince of Wales Hotel, Llanberis, the double-spaced verbatim typescript of the proceedings runs to 69 pages. The first witnesses were passengers who confirmed that Aitchison had called out for them to keep their seats before Roberts jumped off.

Roberts had fallen against the side of a cutting, breaking his right leg and rolling back towards the train. He was not run over but his broken leg was then crushed between the foot-board and the ground. Afterwards he remained conscious but his knee bled heavily. Asked why he had jumped, he had told Aitchison that it was because he had seen the loco crew jumping.

Aitchison explained that the track at the accident site had

been laid in December 1895, that there had been four or five trains a day during construction, which consolidated the track, and that there had been one incident where a loco, No 2, had mounted the rack. In that case No 2 had stopped within 10yd and got on to the rack again without intervention, the incident that Fox had reported to the board in February (p20). He also told the inquest about the derailment of the residents' train on 4 April (p26).

Amadelo Taechella, an Italian mechanical engineer, SLM's representative, had accompanied the first locomotive in June 1895 and had remained to train the loco drivers. He thought the ground, which had been frozen, had settled, allowing the loco to mount the rack. Fox confirmed that there was a slight subsidence in the formation, a depression of about 2in that extended for some distance. Five or six sleepers had been disturbed, but none fractured.

No 1's driver, Pickles, was a Derbyshire man who had moved to Llanberis to work as a driver during the line's construction. Some newspaper reports said that he was from Yorkshire; his fireman was his nephew. He had trained John Sellars, No 2's driver, who was not asked about his origins. Sellars had been No 2's driver when it had left the rack in February, when he and his fireman had also jumped off; the load then had been three laden trucks, although one report said two. He and his fireman had jumped off No 2 before it collided with the carriages on 6 April, too.

Marindin asked a number of questions during proceedings, particularly about the rack and the existence, or otherwise, of devices to prevent the rolling stock from parting company with it.

After deliberating for 40 minutes the jury returned a verdict that the loco had left the rack and the deceased followed the loco crew's example and 'jumped out of the carriage and met his death.' There was not sufficient evidence to show why the locomotive mounted the rack.

Not surprisingly, speculation about the cause of the accident was widespread. On 11 April the *Manchester Guardian* reprinted an article from the *Westminster Gazette* written by an unnamed mountaineer. The writer claimed that during the summer of 1895 a mountain guide had forecast a mishap at the spot where the accident had occurred, reasoning that the railway there was on made-up ground and the ground on which it was founded was naturally unstable, unreliable and 'always shifty'. During the winter strong winds would blow snow into the embankment where it would freeze. The thawing ground would be sodden and likely to sink. On the day of the accident, the writer expounded, the weight of the two trains had caused the ground to sink, enabling the loco to lose contact with the rack and causing the accident.

Mountaineers and their guides were not alone in developing theories about the accident's cause. On 10 April, John Ord, a customs examining officer at Nelson dock, Liverpool, wrote to the Board of Trade that he might be able to shed some light on it and what he saw as the company's attempt to conceal its cause. During the day that he wrote, he had examined a case intended for the railway that contained '24 pieces of machinery apparently intended for brakes'. On enquiring, he established that the locomotives had 'not been furnished with these appliances ... and my suspicions were deepened by the eagerness of the person who applied for the case ... he stated that it was a matter of life and death ... I examined and counted the pieces and secretly marked most of them ... The impression made on me is that these appliances may be attached to the engines ... and the cause of the disaster thus concealed ...'

Writing on 12 April, Marindin said 'I think I can explain ... The two [sic] engines which were in use on the Snowdon

Railway are disabled, one having been broken up. The others which were used in construction work are in the shops for repair. One of them is all right except that the brake blocks are so much worn that the engineer declined to use the engine to take me up to the scene of the accident. The company can do nothing in the direction of clearing the line and bringing down the disabled engine and carriages until they have another engine in perfect order, and they are very anxious for the arrival of the new brake blocks, which they told me last Wednesday were on their way from Switzerland, where the engines were built. They told me at the same [time] they were trying to hasten the delivery, as they had no blocks in store.' So apart from Marindin losing track of the number of locomotives available to the company it was all perfectly innocent.

It was to be a year before the railway was fully opened to passenger traffic. Not only did it become obvious that a great deal of work needed to be done, but it was necessary to ensure that there could be no repeat of the accident. There were compensation claims, the company's capitalisation, and other issues to deal with as well.

The first post-accident SMTH board meeting had been held on 13 April, when the directors heard reports from both Aitchison and Oswell. Aitchison had been instructed to inform the Lancaster Carriage & Wagon Company to postpone work on the carriages on order in case modifications were required, which implies that all six had not been delivered. Approval had also been given to the contractors using locomotive No 3. Before adjourning to visit the accident location, the directors had resolved to express their condolences to Roberts' widow and relatives. Afterwards, the contractors had been instructed to retrieve the damaged rolling stock on the basis that the company would pay until the issue of liability was resolved.

The *Railway Times'* reported on 9 May 1896 that the track had been repaired and made safe. In what was clearly intended to be a demonstration of confidence, Assheton-Smith had even taken a party up the mountain in a special train. In the light of the work required before the line could be opened to the public this report could be considered slightly disingenuous.

On 22 May, the MP for central Finchley laid down a question in the House of Commons, asking the president of the Board of Trade what information he had on the cause of the accident, who certified that the line was safe for traffic, when

any reports would be published and if, and by whom, the line would be tested before being used by holiday traffic? The brief reply ignored Marindin's involvement, saying that as the line was not constructed under any statutory authority, the railways acts did not apply and no passengers would be carried until precautions had been taken to prevent another accident.

A report on the desirability of installing an additional, unspecified, safeguard had been submitted by Fox before the board met on 18 April but, whilst agreeing to adopt it, the directors also wanted him to report on the accident's cause and how their railway differed from the Swiss Abt lines. They also sought his opinion on whether trains should be limited to a single carriage 'when the ballasting is properly completed to his satisfaction.' Fox's report was considered on 5 May and his proposal for adding 'safety angle irons' to the rack adopted. Approval was to be given to employing the Carnarvon ironfounders, de Winton & Company, to 'fix the gripper arrangement on locomotives 2 and 3', on 26 August 1896.

Fox had investigated other mountain lines about the precautions taken to prevent 'rack mounting' and consulted several engineers, including SLM, but not Rinecker, Abt, concerning the practicality of the angle irons and having received their approval, on 16 May the board agreed to tender for its supply, the order to be awarded on price, but taking delivery time into consideration. The president of the Institution of Civil Engineers, Sir Benjamin Baker, who acted for the contractors, gave the angle irons his approval, too. No details were recorded about the tenders received. The minutes of a meeting held on 6 March 1897 refer to a settlement to be made with Dorman, Long & Company, steelmaker of Middlesborough, so that company was probably the supplier.

As news of the modification circulated, questions were asked of Rinecker, Abt & Company, the patentees, about the safety of existing Abt lines. Feeling its reputation slighted and faced with the lack of an inquiry into the accident and its representations to both Fox and the Board of Trade ignored, the company submitted the correspondence to *The Engineer*, which published it on 11 September. Rinecker, Abt had been surprised when Marindin had approved the line for public operation, as on 19 March, their own engineer, Frank B. Passmore, had inspected the line at Fox's request. He had written: 'The ends of the sleepers in many places project beyond the ballast. In other places the ends of the sleepers rest on boulders forming the bottom ballast. In some places where this occurs, and where the sleeper is not packed further along, the end of the sleeper is bent up. I drew attention to this on my last visit. I don't know if the damaged sleepers have been removed but I notice that some of them have not. As, however, many are now covered over with ballast, I cannot speak of those so covered. In many cases I could put my arm halfway up to the elbow under the sleeper ends. In many places you can stand on a sleeper and shake two or three on either side of you. The ballast is far too large, and the sleepers can never be properly packed with it. The ballast in many places is very dirty, and should be taken off, as it will work into the mud to the detriment of the road. I saw one gang putting on soil from the sides to make up ballast. There are a great many places where the alignment is very bad … where the road is low. There are many curves bad [sic]. The change of grade at the downhill side of the Chapel bridge at 1m should be improved …

'I found many of the [rack] bars wrongly spaced… The rack is very dirty. In places the dirt and stones have been pressed in hard by pinions, and if by accident a stone should get in at one of these places, it would very probably throw the engine off the line. Where anchors have been put in, the rack is left covered with cement. The rack should be thoroughly cleaned and cleared of all soil, dirt and ballast, so that if anything gets in it will fall through. The rack should then be well greased, and the ballast should not reach to the bottom of the rack. The rack has been very inefficiently greased, and no oil has been used to lubricate the teeth of the pinions of the engine. The driver's excuse is that the oil freezes. This surely could be obviated by the use of kerosene mixed with the other oil. The result of the ill-usage the rack has received is that it shows more wear than would be represented by a year's proper use of the railway in full working [sic]. There are distinct hollows on the face of the teeth and burrs on the side in many places … in my opinion three-fourths of the line will require to be lifted, straightened and properly packed. Someone … has taken it upon himself to alter the switches supplied by Messrs Cammell & Co and has, of course, spoilt them – in fact they are dangerous in their present state …'

Having the benefit of being written before the accident, this report must be accepted at face value. Quite clearly the track was poorly laid, probably by labourers with no track-laying experience. Passmore's report raises the question of the nature of Marindin's inspection. He did not mention the track. The defects Passmore saw could not be fixed in a week – he estimated two months – and they would have been visible to a walking inspection or to anyone riding in the guard's coupé at the front of the train. One can only imagine that Marindin's inspection was by train and that he travelled in one of the passenger compartments. Whether this was a deliberate ploy by the contractors and/or Aitchison is open to speculation.

Determined that a 'slight subsidence' in the rack would not caused a loco to mount it, Rinecker, Abt had addressed the specifics of the accident location in a letter to the Board of Trade dated 11 June. The company had established that there was a short section of 3.15ch (205ft) where the gradient was 1 in 13.2 between much longer sections of 1 in 6.6, above, and 1 in 5.5. The 1-in-13.2 section it called a step or bench saying: 'It is so short that it is impossible to ease the corners with vertical curves

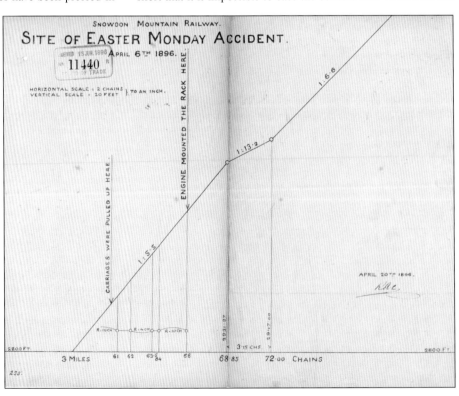

Rinecker, Abt's gradient diagram showing the site of the accident submitted to the Board of Trade.
National Archives

of sufficiently long radii, and the velocity of a down train meets, therefore, with a rapid succession of changes, necessitating also rapid changes in the handling of the different parts of the air brake.

'Close to the lower end of the lower vertical curve, at 3m 66ch, where the line was badly packed, a short length of rail being quite loose, and where the super elevation was quite excessive, we hear that the engine gave a lurch and the pinions mounted the rack, not only of the first train, but also of the train following. It is quite immaterial whether the train descended at a speed of 3.5 to 4mph as it is asserted, or whether it was a little more, since the speed after passing that bench must have increased quite rapidly, and even if the driver did not lock the pinions by closing the handbrake rapidly, then certainly the automatic brake caused the pinions to become locked. The speed of the train was close to the limit of the automatic speed brake when that badly packed spot was passed, and it is therefore possible that by the sudden jerk the automatic brake dropped and locked the pinions ... There is no doubt whatever, but that a pinion can mount the rack only when the speed is checked suddenly by closing the brake too rapidly, and thereby locking the pinion ...

'When all the facts are considered, it must not be overlooked that the accident happened to the first regular train at the opening of the railway; that this first train was composed of two carriages with full load, which is the specified maximum; that the line was entirely new and still in an unfinished and unsettled condition; that the time of the year was rather early and the frost hardly yet out of the ground; that the drivers, able as they may be, could not be supposed to have already acquired sufficient experience at once with a full load.

'None of all these facts point to any defect of the Abt rack system, and it is entirely impossible, therefore, to improve the condition of the railway by the introduction of so-called safety rails, forming, in our opinion, a new element of danger. But all the evidence shows the necessity of removing all the existing causes of accidents, and it should be made a point, in the first instance, that the above-mentioned bench is entirely removed and a steep gradient of about 1 in 7.5 substituted therefore; that the vertical curves are overhauled and flattened as much as possible; that the automatic brake is arranged in such a way that it cannot lock the pinions, or, better still, that it is entirely removed, and that the various faults pointed out by Mr Passmore ... be made good.'

In a letter to Fox dated 16 May, Rinecker, Abt pointed out that guard rails like those proposed had been introduced on the Rigi Railway, which used a ladder rack, 25 years earlier and were quickly found to be ineffective. Despite the Rigi locomotives having only a single driving pinion and gradients as steep as 1 in 4 there had been no accidents. If the railway really must have an additional safeguard, Fox was told, then a brake pinion on the trailing axle worked from an independent handle on the footplate was the answer. It would be less costly and more quickly accomplished.

Rinecker, Abt also pointed out to Fox that on the SMTH only the rack bars had been made to Abt drawings and specifications and under their superintendence. The locomotives, on the other hand, were of an Abt type made for other lines and had been ordered without Rinecker, Abt being consulted. The company had been faced with considerable difficulty in getting the locomotives' heating surface and tank capacity increased to make them suitable for the SMTH.

These two letters surely provide a better explanation for the accident than any other provided. The track quality was poor and the resident engineers had failed to understand that smooth vertical transitions between changing gradients were crucial. Given that it was April and the section of track concerned was sheltered from any sun it is unlikely that there would have been sufficient change in ground temperature to reduce track stability. Several witnesses agreed that the loco had lurched, indicating that the track had moved under it. The descent of the first fully laden two-carriage train almost certainly played a part in what happened, but whether greater experience would have helped the driver is this circumstance is open to question.

If he was to emerge from the SMTH project with his reputation intact, Fox *had* to implement an apparent improvement to the Abt system. He could not admit that the work had been poorly carried out in the first place. That no other Abt railway has found it necessary to install SMTH-style angle irons and grippers speaks for itself.

One further influence on the cause came from the report commissioned by the contractors, from C. A. W. Pownall and Lionel B. Wells, dated 15 July 1896. Quoted in Boyd (see Bibliography), the whereabouts of the original are unknown, Pownall and Wells suggest that the locomotive was 29% overloaded on the downhill journey. 'Having regard to the comparative weights of engines and trains on similar lines, we are of the opinion that, although the Snowdon engines are capable of taking a full load of 18.5 tons uphill, they should be limited when descending to a load not exceeding their own weight.' This remark was going to exercise Aitchison for the next three years.

When an SLM representative visited the line to assess the impact of the angle-iron grippers on the locomotives in December 1896, he was concerned to notice the number of changes in gradient over short distances, saying: 'On these short lengths it is very difficult to adjust the brake resistance so as to obtain a uniform speed especially when they occur in conjunction with curves. If it had been possible to keep the gradients for a greater distance uniform, even at the expense of more earthwork [sic] it would doubtless be an improvement.' Rinecker, Abt's appeal to Fox to ease the vertical curves appeared not to have been put into effect.

Returning to matters at Llanberis, by 16 May 1896 the board had become dissatisfied with the contractors' performance. They had failed to carry out construction and maintenance in a proper and efficient manner and had ignored instructions concerning the use of the locomotive, 'the same having been run over dangerous parts of the line contrary to direct orders.' The blame was directed towards Rigby, the agent, and Fox was to see if he could be sacked. The company also withdrew its consent for the use of locomotives except under controlled conditions. No doubt the contractors were responsible for an incident involving 'No 4 truck' that occurred on 11 June.

A show-down took place between the board and contractor Holme at Fox's London office on 26 June. Holme declared that he intended giving up the contract on 6 July and would allow the company £600 to complete the works. Fox responded that this sum was inadequate 'as so much remained to be done.' Holme replied that only the 'top station', the bridge at 4miles 20ch, some fencing and some side drains remained outstanding and refused to 'do anything towards remedying the tight joints to the rails' – had his men left no expansion gaps? Asked if he would complete the line to specification and defer the matter of liability for payment to arbitration he refused. After Holme had left the meeting, Fox was asked to take legal advice with a view of serving the contractors with 21 days' notice to complete the tramroad and to supply lists of the outstanding construction work and the outstanding maintenance.

The notice was served on 1 July and the contractors replied on 24 July. The letter was read out at a directors' meeting, and

Right: **A 1952 view of the Padarn Villa Hotel; acquired by the SMTH as part of a compensation deal agreed with Roberts's widow, it was sold in 1920.** *Valentine/ Author's collection*

Below right: **Advertisements for both the Padarn Villa and Victoria hotels in the *Carnarvon & Denbigh Herald* published in May 1896.**

at an extraordinary general meeting of shareholders that followed, the next day. Details of their proposal were not recorded but as they were acceptable to Fox they were approved. Holme had told the shareholders that he had the largest holding and was the 'one mainly responsible for the scheme'. At the directors' meeting Aitchison was 'instructed to consult with the engineers and report as to how the work of carrying on the contract should be done after 1 August.'

Tidying up after the contractors started. Rigby was still on-site and was not to be given any facilities. The company agreed to take a Whitworth rail-cutting machine against the contract, but did not want a shed as it had no use for it. Although Oswell was instructed to employ a man to carry out the outstanding work, completion of the construction was actually carried out under Aitchison's supervision.

While Fox had claimed that the track was undamaged by the accident, on 16 May the directors had ordered that it should be 'thoroughly repaired and all the damaged rack bars removed where injured …' Cammell's tender for 300 rack bars and bolts and sleepers was to be accepted on 13 June. As the rack bars were 1.8m long, allowing for the double rack this gives a length of up to 270m that had been damaged. The Press Association's account of the accident published in the *Leeds Mercury* on 8 April had stated that 'much damage has been done to the track for about 200yd.'

Fox did not totally escape the directors' criticism, being told after their 13 June meeting that 'the directors regretted not having Mr Rowlandson's report placed before them'. Rowlandson had presumably been consulted on the cause or solution to the accident; possibly he was Charles Arthur Rowlandson of the Manchester, Sheffield & Lincolnshire Railway.

Aitchison's scheme for installing a second independent brake on the carriages was approved by the board on 6 March 1897, when he was given permission to consult with Fox on the subject.

On the subject of compensation and other expenses arising from the accident, the directors agreed, on 28 April, that Roberts' executor's claim 'should have careful and sympathetic consideration … the company do not admit any liability, also to ask for a basis to work upon before making any offer [of compensation].' Roberts had been the proprietor of the Padarn Villa Hotel. Despite it being quite clear that he had sustained injury because he disobeyed Aitchison's instruction to remain seated, the board felt some obligation to compensate his widow, and on 16 May it agreed to buy the hotel for £2,547, a sum that included £550 compensation. The purchase was completed on 23 May.

Other claims were made by H. Jackson of Oswestry – which was repudiated, as the company would pay his doctor's bill – and H. E. Smith of Bristol, whose claim was refused outright. Jackson tried for more, to be told in June that the company's final offer was £20 inclusive of his medical expenses. The Dinorwic quarry doctor's bill of £10 10s was accepted in June as he had been called in by Aitchison. A second doctor was offered £3 3s without prejudice, the company eventually settling for £5 5s.

A claim for shock alleged to have been sustained by a Miss Ethel Kilshaw was lodged with the company on 21 August, the directors resolving that it could not be entertained owing to the time that had elapsed. It was to be settled for £170 at Liverpool assizes on 17 March 1897, Miss Kilshaw's ability to employ a QC evidently being to her advantage.

In the circumstances, the company escaped lightly for it obviously had no public liability insurance. On 6 March 1897, the directors approved an agreement with the Railway Passengers Assurance Company 'for insuring the company against damage to passengers by accidents …'

To complete the company's capitalisation, a call for £25 per debenture and the final call of £1 per share on the post-16 August issues were to be paid by 9 June 1896. Aitchison was to apply for a listing on the Manchester stock exchange as well as the Liverpool exchange. The listing at the latter was in place by 9 July, when a further £25 call on the debentures was agreed. By November, 7,000 £10 shares had been allocated although £2,250 remained unpaid, while £19,000 of debentures had been issued, of which £1,750 was unpaid. The balance sheet gave a figure of £71,946 7s 10d for construction, 'including estimated cost of accident'. The hotels and Llanberis refreshment room had cost £6,303 17s 4d.

Some minutiæ dealt with on 13 June 1896 included the station refreshment room, presumably at Llanberis, to be opened as soon as the building was completed, and the names of the two new locomotives: No 4 to be *Snowdon* and No 5 to be *Moel Siabod*. At the extraordinary shareholders' meeting to be held on 25 July Fox was to report that 'the fourth locomotive has been passed, and the fifth will be ready for despatch by August'. Aitchison was authorised to run a train for a party of Royal Engineer officers and instructors on 22 June, at the travellers' risk.

Tenders for building the summit hotel from Owen Morris of Carnarvon (£6,992) and Younger of Birkenhead (£5,600) were also considered on 13 June. It is likely that the Carnarvon bid was more realistic and took account of the extra costs of working on the mountain. Neither was accepted and Aitchison was to recruit a clerk of works to construct the building by piece work. On 9 July, the hotel was deferred until the tramroad was completed and Fox was asked to design a timber building to occupy a site at the summit identified by the county surveyor. Morris's subsequent tender of £367 for this work was also considered excessive. An offer to buy the Bulkeley estate's summit hut was refused on 6 March 1867 as the price, £1,500, was also considered too much.

The board obviously thought that Aitchison had acquitted himself well, for on 28 April 1896 it increased his salary to £400 and paid him £30 in respect of his accommodation during the previous year. On 6 March 1897, the directors then resolved to transfer £150 from the share account to be paid to him as part-payment for his services in completing the contract work. On the same occasion his salary was increased to £450 and ½% of gross takings and his employment was made subject to six months' notice on either side.

Operation of revenue-earning trains had been considered by the directors on 1 October 1896 and Aitchison was given discretion to start a service as far as Waterfall. No more was said at the board but Aitchison had already, on 16 September, informed the Board of Trade that a section of 'safety angle irons' had been laid and grippers attached to the locomotives and that the company wished to start a service as far as the angle irons extended; was it intended to re-inspect the line? He was notified by letter dated 23 September that the Board of Trade had no desire to order a re-inspection. On 29 September, the *Northern Echo* reported that services to Waterfall had been started and on 3 October *Railway Times* recorded that 'frequent trips are being run.' Aitchison also had discretion to decide when the service should be discontinued for the winter.

The lack of board meetings between 1 October 1896 and 6 March 1897 suggests that there was little activity requiring the directors' attention. On the latter occasion they approved an agreement with the Snowdon Summit Hotel Company Ltd (SSHC) concerning the carriage of goods on the tramroad during 1897. SSHC was probably a joint venture between Assheton-Smith and Sir Richard Bulkeley, the summit landowners. The directors also resolved that 'The line be opened for traffic for

Easter if possible subject to Sir Douglas Fox's approval – the trains to run only as far as the state of the weather and line will permit.'

Prepared for the company's annual meeting on 6 April 1897 (surely not deliberately the anniversary of the accident), the annual report revealed that the company was in dispute with the contractors over the cost of completing the line. Fox's report stated that good progress had been made with completing the line under Aitchison's supervision and that the 'safeguard' was completed to within half a mile of the summit. The works, including the summit station, should be completed a short time after snow cleared.

The directors also met on 6 April and considered a letter from Francis Fox dated 1 April. He said that he had been as far as 4miles 20ch in a train with Aitchison. Deep snow had been cleared and the safeguard fitted to that point. He saw no reason why the railway should not be opened to Clogwyn at Easter, 'and to the summit as soon afterwards as the weather allows Mr Aitchison to do the necessary work.' Fox continued: 'I think he has made a great improvement in the line, especially looking to the manner in which Mr Rigby did the work originally. And not only has he done it very well but at a very reasonable cost.' The summit station, Fox explained, could not be recommenced until the snow had cleared; the weather had pulled the partially erected buildings into odd shapes as the roof had not been fixed before the winter.

The directors authorised Aitchison to open the railway for traffic as far as Clogwyn 'on or after Monday next' and to the summit as soon as the line was complete. After a discussion with Holme, the directors decided that Fox should certify the amount, if any, due to the contractors and the amount to be deducted by the company for 'work omitted or done inefficiently by the contractor.' Aitchison was also instructed to draw up the company's statement of counterclaim.

An early train, the carriage roofboards are in place, on the viaduct above the waterfalls. *Frith/Author's collection*

Snowdon Travelogue

Photographs by the author except where stated otherwise

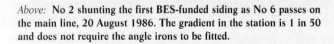

Above: No 2 shunting the first BES-funded siding as No 6 passes on the main line, 20 August 1986. The gradient in the station is 1 in 50 and does not require the angle irons to be fitted.

Above right: A modern scene at Llanberis station, viewed from the lifting gantry on 28 September 1996.

Right: No 11 climbs the 1-in-8 gradient on the Afon Hwch Viaduct on 21 June 1996.

Below: Half a mile from Llanberis, at Waterfall station the gradient eases from 1 in 6 to 1 in 20. No 12 and carriage No 3 were in operation on 11 July 1999.

Left: **The scene on 11 July 1999 from near Waterfall, as two trains cross at Hebron station, left. The station is named after Capel Hebron, visible to the right. The summit is visible on the upper right of the picture.**

Middle: **No 6 climbing to Hebron on 11 July 1999. Behind the train are the abandoned galleries of the Dinorwic slate quarries.**

Bottom left: **A train climbs towards Hebron on 12 July 1999. Waterfall station is on the right.**

Below: **Two railways in one picture. The 2ft gauge Llanberis Lake Railway runs alongside Llyn Padarn, the backdrop to this view of No 2 on 11 July 1999.**

Left: **The groundframe dominates this view of No 9 and carriage No 7 at Hebron, on 19 August 1989. Just over 1 mile from Llanberis, the gradient changes from 1 in 6 to 1 in 10.**

Above: **Still at Hebron some two hours later, No 9 is returning to Llanberis and No 2 has arrived on test after receiving attention in the workshop.**

Above: **Loco No 4 and carriage No 4 at Hebron in September 1991. The first wind turbine is on the right.**

Right: **On 29 September 2000 No 5 makes a fine display as it crosses the footpath below Halfway. Two miles from Llanberis, the gradient is 1 in 6.** *John Kenward*

Above: Hebron seen on 1 September 1992, a 'new' wind turbine is surrounded by a security compound, as the first was stolen during the winter of 1991/2. Almost the full extent of Llyn Padarn and its environs can be seen in this photograph of No 11 and one of the SIS carriages.

Below: During 1970, No 3 and carriage No 6 have just crossed the footpath and are about to enter the cutting below Halfway. The carriage is decorated with crests on the body panels and above the front windscreen. *Edward Dorricott*

Below: The latest installation at Hebron seen from the train on 11 June 2009. There are two wind turbines and solar panels, and the signals use LEDs. On the uphill journey the top points are changed by the guard using a remote control, the driver having that responsibility on the way down.

Left: A modern train about to enter the loop at Halfway, No 10 and carriage No 10 on 10 August 1989. The carriage had just entered service. At 2¼ miles from Llanberis, the gradient here is 1 in 11.

Top: **Two trains ascending, a doubler in SMR-speak, at Halfway on 22 August 1999. No 4 takes water while No 9 and carriage No 7 wait behind. In the background, a train returns to Llanberis. The station's wind turbine is on the right.**

Above left: **A guard's-eye view of Halfway station on 12 June 2009, complete with wind turbine, solar panels and LED signals. No 9 has charge of the down train. Beyond the station the gradient increases to 1 in 6.6.**

Above right: **No 5 and carriage No 3 roll downhill, having just passed No 2 with carriage No 2 at Halfway on 4 May 1999.**

Left: **High winds are usually the reason for terminating trains at Rocky Valley halt; on 13 April 1998 the reason was snow. No 4 arrives with carriage No 4.**

Above: **Doublers near Rocky Valley on 6 April 1996; members of the permanent way gang hitch a lift to Clogwyn.**

Above: **A few paces to the left and the view of the same ensemble is completely different. The current health and safety climate has put an end to the practice of personnel riding on the outside of trains.**

Above: **Nos 6 and 8 at Clogwyn in May 1977. Just over 3¼ miles from Llanberis, there is 3ch with a gradient of 1 in 15.**

Left: **To be at Clogwyn and watching ascending trains is a bizarre sensation, amplified when there are doublers, because the trains come into and go out of view and appear to be travelling in opposite directions. On 4 April 1996, No 4 and carriage No 5 take centre stage while another train, which is actually in front, can hardly be seen.**

Above left: **The Dinorwic slate quarries come into view again near Clogwyn, forming a backdrop for a pair of railcars on 6 April 1996.**

Above right: **Trains that terminate at Clogwyn run through the loop to give passengers access to the platform, providing the opportunity for this view where the station is seen from, and reflected in, the train on 6 April 1996.**

Right: **Decorated by its driver, who also added features to mark the railway's centenary, No 4 was photographed at Clogwyn on 6 April 1996, almost to the minute of that fateful accident 100 years previously. The 20ch of snow-filled cutting behind is on a gradient of 1 in 5.5, with the 15ch section approach to the summit, the steepest parts of the line.**

Below: **Trains approaching Clogwyn, seen from another train on 12 July 1999. The station has solar panels, but is too exposed for wind turbines.**

Above: Cwellyn forms the backdrop as No 2 climbs to the summit on 12 July 1999.

Left: No 2 at the summit in the early 1960s; the carriage is still painted brown. *Mervyn Mason*

Below: Nos 9 and 4 at the summit station on 11 August 1989. The building has been refurbished and re-equipped by the Snowdonia National Park Authority and was said to be 80% efficient.

4

Regular operations

Easter Monday 1897 fell on 19 April. The *North Wales Chronicle* reported that Aitchison ran a pilot train to the summit at 8am and, finding everything satisfactory, the first of five trains left for Clogwyn at 10.45, the last leaving at 2pm and returning to Llanberis at 5pm, when it rained heavily. Each train consisted of just a locomotive and one carriage, 'it is intended to adhere to this arrangement for some weeks to come, if not permanently.' A longer report on the day's activities in the *Carnarvon & Denbigh Herald*, repeated in other publications in a briefer form, claimed that £9,000 had been spent on the safety rail and that it had been adapted by several Swiss railways, the latter almost certainly wishful thinking. The reporters were shown No 1's boiler, where the only visible damage was a slight dent; it would be surprising if some of its stays had not broken.

The *Daily News* reported that it had been snowing when Aitchison's train reached the summit, and the *Glasgow Herald* reported that it had been carrying provisions, furniture and coal for the hotel; the latter also reported that snow drifts 14ft deep had prevented the angle irons being laid to the summit.

John Partington, of the LNWR audit office, visited during the summer of 1897 and his account was published in *The Railway Magazine*. The train comprised a locomotive and carriage, the seats of which were not upholstered; the Webb-Thompson electric staff controlled the single line; at Clogwyn it was intended to build walls or an arched way to protect the

trains from storms, and the summit station building was unfinished. A GPO post box was located at the summit and the train that carried the mail ran non-stop to Llanberis. One of his fellow travellers had been Sir Edward Watkin, owner of the Hafod y Llan estate, which included a part of the summit, and former chairman of the Great Central Railway, then aged 78. Not for the first time apparently, he was carried to the summit inn by the driver and guard in a sedan chair.

A photographic souvenir, possibly published in 1897, stated that the intermediate stopping places were located at 'near Ceunant Mawr (the Waterfall)', 'near the Methodist chapel', 'opposite the first halfway house' and at 'Clogwyn, near Cyrn Las' and that passengers could book to or from them. Summarising the railway's history, the guide mentioned the first train to the summit on 8 January 1896 and then, with classic understatement, 'After this there was a delay, and it was not until April 1897 that the line was completely open …'

Now that the railway was operating, the main issue facing the directors was settling the dispute with the contractors. On 8 May, they offered to separate the Kilshaw claim from the construction dispute by suggesting that each party should pay

A train awaits departure at Llanberis in the early years with one of the wagons in the siding and stores for the summit on the platform. *Author's collection*

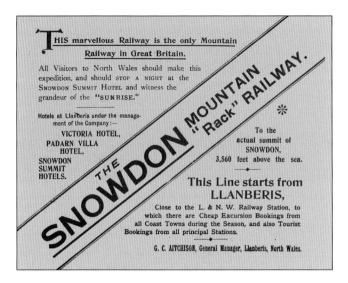

half of the settlement. The directors refused to accept the contractors' suggestion, and were understandably cross about it, that Fox should act as arbitrator.

Just how the arbitration was proceeded with is not clear but a preliminary agreement made on 6 July was signed on 12 July. Under its terms the contractors accepted £5,029 12s 4d, less £744 16s 4d in settlement of the contract, and £281 16s 9d in discharge of all accounts against the company. All the costs and damages in connection with the Kilshaw claim were to be pooled and the contractors and the company were to pay half each; the contractors were to pay their calls on debentures and shares.

This seems like a poor deal for SMHT, with the contractors paying only £744 16s 4d for the poor workmanship, if that is the correct interpretation, and nothing at all in respect of the accident. When the company's balance sheet was prepared for the annual report in November 1897, £76,430 18s 8d had been spent on construction and £1,942 2s 2d on preliminary expenses and the 'cost of reconstructing line after accident'. Even if Fox was paid 10% on the contract cost, the contractors appeared to have done well out of their £64,000 fixed-price contract. By 1899, incidentally, the cost of construction and reconstruction had settled at £75,952 11s 7d and £2,292 2s 2d, which figures were then repeated in each year's annual report.

Fox, too, should not have escaped without criticism, although he seems to have done. He and his resident engineer certainly should have done something about the sloppy trackwork. When he sought payment for extra work in July

1897 the board would only sanction £200, the balance due to him under the contract.

Having been critical of the original trackwork it should be noted that the contractors' structures have lasted well. The most substantial, the viaducts, have required very little consideration over years and stand as memorials to their work. Elsewhere, only the bridge abutments have received attention and at Llanberis the station buildings and locomotive shed remain in use.

On 8 May, Aitchison was told to investigate having an open carriage built. The cost must have been too much, and would not have been much different from the cost of the semi-open vehicles already in the fleet, for in November a carriage was *sent* to Lancaster Carriage & Wagon Company for evaluation. On 18 January 1898 the board approved payment of £50 10s to have it altered. It was returned without its roof and reduced in length. The alteration might have been a consequence of the remark made by Pownall and Wells (p33) that the locomotives were overloaded on the downhill journey. Could the carriage chosen have been that which No 2 had collided with on 6 April 1896? If, as seems likely, only peak service trains were run with two carriages then the one most badly damaged might have been left unrepaired.

The 1897 annual report stated that between 11,000 and 12,000 passengers were carried during the railway's first full year of operation, producing a profit of £499 4s 3d after the payment of £342 0s 5d debenture interest. A loss of £1,388 0s 8d was carried forward.

Top left: **An early advertisement for the SMTH.** *Author's collection*

Top right: **The cover of what might have been the first SMTH guide. Although the location is easily identifiable, the train is quite unlike any that has run on the railway.** *Author's collection*

Left: **A view of the LNWR's Llanberis station from the footbridge shows, from left, Dolbadarn Castle, the Victoria Hotel and the SMR terminus. As a part of the hotel's estate, the castle was owned by the SMR, *c*1900.** *Pictorial Stationery Company/ Author's collection*

A panorama that shows the Victoria Hotel and exterior of the SMR station. *Photochrom/Author's collection*

When a second application had been made to Portmadoc licensing sessions for a licence at the summit in September 1897, Aitchison had said that 9,700 tickets had been issued between Easter and the end of August. The *North Wales Chronicle's* report of the proceedings explained that there were already two licensed premises on the summit: the hotel company's, a timber structure with a galvanised iron roof, and the 'original hut', Roberts's. Aitchison explained that the SMTH hotel would have 14 bedrooms and accommodate 200 diners. The hotel company's barrister called the application speculative because SMTH did not produce any witnesses claiming that the existing provision was inadequate. On 20 June, the night of Queen Victoria's Golden Jubilee, 14 people had stayed at the summit. After the barrister representing Beddgelert Parish Council and the Watkin Estate got into an argument with the chairman of the bench, the license was refused following a 10-minute adjournment. In September SSHC obtained approval to increase the number if its bedrooms fron four to seven

One of the features of Swiss mountain railways that Aitchison had noticed was that passengers could send telegrams and postcards announcing their presence at the summit. On 1 May 1896 he had written to the GPO suggesting that a public telegraph station be opened on the summit. In April 1897, the hotel company also offered to provide a service by taking over an existing line to Glanaber, Nant Gwynant, which had been installed and then abandoned by Sir Edward Watkin. The latter was refused on 28 August 1897, the same date that SMTH was told that its proposal was accepted, the GPO offering to pay 2d commission per telegram accepted and to provide a 'handing-over' circuit between SMTH premises and Llanberis Post Office, probably a cheaper option than connecting to the Watkin cable.

Despite the directors agreeing to the GPO's contract on 29 September 1897, and it being made on 4 June 1898, Aitchison wrote on 13 August appealing for the telegraph office to be opened as soon as possible, saying: 'We hope a large and plain sign or two will be supplied calling attention to the telegraph office. The name of the station is "Snowdon Summit" station. Can this stamp be affixed to letters at present written on the summit, some scores per diem.' A notice announcing the opening of the station for 'the transaction of public telegraph business … when the line is working' was placed in the *Post Office Circular* on 17 August and the date stamp was ordered. Aitchison was informed that it was not policy to supply signs; the separate reply concerning the stamping of postcards has not survived.

During the course of negotiations the GPO had noticed that SMTH had charges for 'to carry and bring down a letter bag, @ per day 6d' and 'letters sent separately 1d', both in breach of its monopoly.

Two minor issues remained outstanding from the line's construction and reconstruction. In January 1898, Assheton-Smith complained that the railway had taken more land than agreed and wanted a survey to be made. The directors agreed to support the survey and said that if the railway had taken more land then the boundaries should be relocated to reduce the amount concerned. Sounding slightly aggrieved, they told Aitchison to point out that they were not to blame if more land had been taken. Revised boundaries were agreed in March 1899.

Arising from the reconstruction, it appears that Oswell, Fox's agent, had obtained a patent for the angle iron. When Fox asked for £50 on Oswell's behalf in May 1858, the directors noted that Oswell was employed by Fox, who was therefore responsible for paying him, and deferred responding until November. Then they agreed to tell Fox that 'as commission has been paid on the angle iron there is no reason … to make any payment to Mr Oswell and that Mr Oswell applied to the board before patenting the angle iron which was designed for their use

Inside the station a train waits to depart. The ground frame that controlled the points and signals is behind the flagpole. The positioning of the beer barrels to the right of the fence suggests that they are empty. *John Alsop Collection*

Left: **Looking down on the upper viaduct. The loco shed and station buildings can be seen beyond it.** *John Alsop Collection*

Below: **No 5 climbs the upper viaduct. The back of Waterfall station is just above the right-hand end of the train.** *SMR*

and was informed that they had no objection as far as its use by other lines was concerned.' Fox had been paid £132 8s 5d for his part in supplying the angle iron in September. It is unlikely that Oswell made any money from his patent.

To accommodate the company's offices, the property called Ty Club was purchased from Assheton-Smith in October 1897. Aitchison's proposals for modifications were subject to an inspection by the directors.

The application to license its proposed summit premises having been refused, SMTH took steps to acquire control of the existing sites there. The Snowdon Summit Hotel Company offered to lease or sell its premises in November, but before accepting, the

directors obtained Assheton-Smith's approval for 'a small building on the existing site in front of the hut and allow the wall to be demolished.' The ground rent, £20 for all of Assheton-Smith's rights on the summit, including Roberts' portion of the hut, was agreed in January 1898. A lease was agreed with Sir Richard Bulkeley for 'his portion of the original summit hut and surrounding land' for 21 years at £7 annually, and Roberts' licence was transferred to Aitchison, as SMTH's secretary. A repairing lease for 14 years, at £160 annually, on the hotel company's property was decided in February and Isaac Newton & Company's tender of £388 for a new building excluding the foundations, to be erected on the site of Roberts' hut was approved in March. The building was completed by July, when it and its contents were insured for £700.

In January 1898 Aitchison was instructed to obtain a £1,200 overdraft from Lloyds Bank to pay for Roberts' hut and the new building. One or more directors had to sign the guarantee and £1,500 debentures were deposited as surety in February. Aitchison was to be instructed to withdraw both the guarantee and the debentures in March 1900.

The Snowdon Summit Hotel Company's lease included an option for SMTH to buy the property for £3,250. During 1911, SSHC was to offer to sell for £1,625, half price. Following some six months of negotiation by Aitchison, SMTH bought the summit hotel in 1912, paying £1,100 which included the furniture and effects; the draft contract was signed on

20 January and the cheque was issued on 11 May. Voluntary liquidation of the hotel company was started in June and was completed in January 1916.

Returning now to March 1898, a demand from the Inland Revenue Board for 5% passenger duty on SMTH's gross passenger receipts, in compliance with the 1842 Regulation of Railways Act, as amended, must have come as quite a shock to the directors. In May, Holme, the contractor and since 12 March a director, replacing Paget, was to use his influence with unidentified MPs to resolve it, but failed. In November, the directors instructed the company's solicitor to say that the company was not liable for the duty and to compromise by offering to pay duty on 3d per mile, the same rate as the LNWR. By January 1899, Aitchison had obtained counsel's opinion on the issue and the directors resolved to issue a cheque for 5% on 3d per mile for the solicitor to pass to the revenue, saying that the remainder of the fare was to be treated as payment for use of the company's grounds and shelters and for access to the mountain. No other details of the settlement were recorded except that in November 1899 the directors signed a bond in favour of the revenue to guarantee that the duty would be paid in future.

The need to arrange an overdraft to buy the summit lease and to pay for the building there indicates that the company was short of funds. In January 1898, the 'financial position' was given as the reason for refusing Aitchison permission to

Right: **Having passed Waterfall and crossed the bridge over Afon Ceunant Bach the train heads to Hebron, visible in the upper centre of the photograph.** *Pictorial Stationery Company/ Author's collection*

Below: **A train with the Lancaster carriage that was shortened and converted into an open. The rivets where the two ends of the underframe were joined together are quite prominent.** *SMR*

commission an illustrated poster to promote the railway. A small improvement to finances was made in March, when the sale of the boiler of 'No 1 engine' for £190 was approved. In May, when there would have been some traffic revenue, a coloured poster and £10 of advertising in the *Birmingham Daily News* were authorised. A search of the British Library's newspaper catalogue suggests that the newspaper's title was wrongly recorded. In May 1899, 1,000 more coloured posters were to be ordered at a cost of £19 5s.

Another financial matter was discussed on 9 July 1898, when Aitchison reported on 'irregularities of abstracting small monies that had occurred'; North was to be given the option of retiring in one week, which implies that he was guilty of theft, but, unless there is an error in the minutes, he remained in charge of the refreshment room. J. Owen was promoted from the summit station to Llanberis station and J. Hayes was transferred to the summit.

Aitchison's involvement with other Welsh railways started in March 1898, when he reported to the board that he had 'unexpectedly and without any wish on his part received the offer of the managership of the North Wales Narrow Gauge Railways.' The directors gave their approval provided that he made an undertaking that 'the interests of the company are not injuriously affected' and made arrangements for the supervision of operations in his absence.

The agreement made with Saunders & Company for maintenance of the signalling system in September 1898 required a special clause that might have been unique to the SMTH and which recognised the railway's special circumstances; SMTH was to provide the labour to re-erect 'any posts blown down'. The 14-year contract cost £25 per annum. In May 1900 Saunders were to propose replacing the overhead wires on 'the top section' with a cable at a cost of £67, an idea that the directors accepted. In June 1901 a return earth wire was to be installed, between the summit and Clogwyn at a cost of £4 10s.

There are no records relating to the number of telegrams sent from the summit following the 1898 agreement with the GPO, but it was perhaps a reflection of changing preferences that in 1901 the company made arrangements for the sale of postage stamps there. Thereafter, many thousands of picture postcards were sold stamped with a 'Summit of Snowdon' cachet. The price of the ½d postage stamp was included in the cost of postcards sold from February 1906.

Seeking to modernise his written communications, in January 1899 Aitchison received approval to purchase a typewriter 'for the office'. He thought a Yost was the most suitable model.

In September 1899 Aitchison reported that 'various renewals of parts' of the locomotives would be required during the winter but that the locomotives would need to be lifted before the necessary parts could be identified.

This is the only reference to the locomotives in the minutes at this time, but Aitchison had been trying to resolve the issue of their capability raised in 1896. Although the entirety of his researches has not survived, a letter to him from Holme dated 3 August 1897 on the subject is indicative of continuing interest. Concluding, 'I trust my notes are legible', Holme supplied information from a book about the Rigibahn. On 12 July 1899 Aitchison submitted his report to Banner. 'I have now in my

possession what purports to be a copy of the contract between Messrs Holme & King and the Winterthur Company. [It is] Dated December 1894.

'*From it* it appears the engines were never ever designed or intended to do the work they were asked to do at the start. As neither the line was designed or constructed with a gradient (maximum) as specified nor were the carriages built to the requisite weight or the number of passengers limited to the number intended.

'I send you a comparative report based on the *supposition* that the copy I have is correct in its details. I have also written the Swiss firm to ask if Messrs Sir Douglas Fox knew of these particulars and approved and I am writing the Lancaster Carriage & Wagon Company to ask if they had any instructions as to the limit of weight.'

SLM's locomotive specification, not included in the Fox volume, had contained a guaranteed performance clause: 'The engines must be capable of driving a load consisting of two cars and passengers up a maximum incline of 18% at a speed 6-7 kilometres per hour, the weight of each car empty being estimated at 4,500Kg and the load due to passengers at 7,800Kg ...'

Aitchison converted the figures: 18% gradient = 1 in 6, and 4,500Kg = 4tons 8cwt 2qtr 8lb 13oz. The steepest SMTH gradient is 1 in 5½, the carriages weighed 5 ton 10cwt 3qtr. He discovered that the weight of passengers was calculated on an average of 75Kg, 52 persons per carriage, 104 per train. SMTH carriages accommodated 56 passengers plus the guard and four more passengers in the coupé. With regards to the gradient he said that the Swiss mountain railway engineers and locomotive builders had a maxim: that an engine had to do twice the work taking two cars up 1 in 5 as in taking one car up 1 in 6. He summarised: 'The gradient is steeper, the carriages are heavier and the carriages hold more passengers than was ever contemplated ... or the locomotives were designed [for].'

He wrote to SLM and on 19 July was told that the builder had not had a performance agreement with the contractors, neither had they corresponded with Fox about it. On 8 August 1894 the contractors had, however, given SLM a specification stating that the maximum gradient would be 1 in 5½ and the train would consist of a locomotive and two carriages carrying about 56 passengers. 'The locomotives we offered were in many respects altered by Messrs Rinecker, Abt & Company and so,

after all, we had to furnish locos different from those we offered at the beginning.'

So it seems that Rinecker, Abt had more influence on the locomotives than they claimed in 1896. There is no written record of the outcome to Aitchison's report and its associated correspondence, but the physical consequence is clear to see: from this date, two full-sized carriages have not been used.

By the end of the 1899 season the company had a positive balance, of £30 13s 5d, to carry forward for the first time. In September, Aitchison had been told to keep the line open until 4 October with discretion to react to demand thereafter; the minimum revenue per train was to be £3 3s. In November he informed the directors that 'if it was intended that a second open car should be ordered for next season no time should be lost as all the works were so busy he had … so far failed to get drawings or estimates.' The shareholders were told that the carriage was 'to enable the increasing traffic to be dealt with more easily.' No details were recorded concerning the carriage's manufacturer, but Boyd (see Bibliography) thought that it was the Ashbury Carriage & Wagon Company in Manchester; it was delivered in 1900.

With the railway operating smoothly and covering its costs the directors met less often, seven meetings in 1899 being followed by four in 1900. In consequence there is less information available about the railway and its operation.

Reverend H. Adler, of Craven Hill, Hyde Park, travelled on the 12.10pm from Llanberis on 29 August 1898. At Halfway the wind was 'somewhat strong' so the guard drew back the curtains, explaining that it would otherwise be too dangerous to proceed further. 'When we arrived at the spot the carriage oscillated violently and there seemed an imminent risk of the train being hurled down.' The train was immediately reversed and the passenger's imaginings came to nought. 'But,' he wrote to the Board of Trade from his accommodation at Llanfairfechan, 'there must be a terrible liability to accidents on a line on which the safety of a train is dependent on the drawing back of curtains, and where a not excessive gust of wind can exercise the effect I experienced today. There were over 30 passengers on the train, many of them being greatly alarmed.'

Aitchison's response to the Board of Trade added more to the story. Previous trains that day had left Llanberis at 7.30am (eight passengers), 10.15am (11) and 11.9am (88) and had completed their journeys in a satisfactory manner. After the 12.10pm departure, on which Adler travelled with 41 others, the

No 4 waits at Clogwyn for a down train to pass. A draught excluder has been fitted to No 4's cabside opening.
John Alsop Collection

weather 'became boisterous' and the train returned to Halfway where it met the 12.54pm departure. As the wind was easing, passengers were given the choice of continuing to the summit on the 12.45pm or returning to Llanberis on the 12.10pm. As it was raining only five chose to continue to the summit. Finding Aitchison at Llanberis, Adler, 'in a very excited state', demanded a full refund. Being offered the difference between the journey he had paid for and the journey he had taken, he refused, saying that he would sue the company. A copy of Aitchison's reply was sent to Adler and nothing more was heard from him.

Aitchison's report that 88 passengers travelled on the 11.9am is confirmation that the use of some two-carriage trains continued after the line had been re-opened.

The number of claims made to SMTH was small in relation to the numbers carried and it was to be 50 years before another passenger complained to officialdom. In September 1899, meanwhile, a Mr Reynolds wanted compensation for hurting his finger while opening a window in the summit hotel, the claim being rejected 'owing to the act being a voluntary one on his part.' Faced with further representations, in November the directors resolved to offer £5 'without prejudice', which Reynolds accepted.

Arriving at Llanberis in October 1899, another visitor had an unexpected experience when he was told that a train could not be run solely for him and his wife. They had travelled 37 miles (from Rhyl?) on the strength of a timetable handbill that indicated that certain trains required a minimum number of passengers to run. The 1.42pm was not one of them, but the booking office clerk 'coolly informed' him that four passengers were required before it would be run. The visitor did not make a formal complaint to the railway, preferring to write to the *North Wales Chronicle* instead.

The next time passengers' complaints were dealt with by the directors was on 9 September 1912. Claiming £2 15s, one passenger had written that he and his wife had travelled on one of the open cars when 'owing to the force and direction of the wind a hot cinder was blown from the loco's chimney and dropped between the claimant and his wife, burning a hole in both their coats.' A Mr J. Gray claimed a refund of 10s, the cost of two tickets from Llandudno, because on 3 September, 'owing to force of wind' the train could not make the complete ascent; the other passengers had accepted a 1s refund in respect of the incomplete journey. Gray had refused it and demanded the full amount. Both claims were settled in full; the author cannot help but be sceptical about the first, given that apparently it was not reported at the time and no evidence was submitted.

Devices to attract revenue and traffic were constantly being sought. In January 1900 the directors agreed to a 'photographic studio' being erected on ground near the river bridge at Llanberis by L. C. Symonds, a local photographer, and to the erection of an advertising board by the LNWR goods entrance, both on terms to be arranged. Symonds agreed to pay £5 5s annually for five years. In 1911, a Mr Francis of Carnarvon offered £18 for the bookstall rights at the summit and was told that if he sold fewer postcards than the average of the previous three years he would receive no commission; otherwise he would be paid 20%. From 11 May 1912 the price of postcards was reduced to 2d, from 3d.

Only generalisations about traffic were made in the annual reports. From these it quickly, and obviously, becomes clear that traffic was very weather-dependent. Before 1914, poor weather was noted as affecting traffic and revenue in 1900, 1901, 1903 and 1908. In 1900 an increase in working expenses was also blamed on increased fuel prices, a not unfamiliar excuse in the early 21st century.

At Llandudno, a kiosk promoted the railway and offered tickets for sale. Discounted tickets were made available to tour operators, including the Polytechnic Touring Association and Messrs Cook & Company. Holme was always keen to arrange advertising in Liverpool and Manchester newspapers but the other directors did not always agree with his proposals, especially in his absence. In May 1911, the directors rejected the Cambrian Railways' proposal to offer through bookings as 'we are unable to accept through bookings from the LNWR.' The value attached to the business brought by the Llandudno charabanc drivers may be judged by the award to them of a present of 10s each on 9 September 1911.

Considering the practicalities of re-opening at Easter, in January 1902 the directors took the pragmatic view that 'Owing to heavy snow and the poor traffic at Easter and during April in previous years the manager was authorised not to trouble to cut out the railway or open for Easter unless circumstances changed and he considered it advisable to do so.' On 12 March 1904, the directors decided to run one train a day during April, except on Easter Monday and Tuesday, 'as far as the snow will permit without digging out.'

The prospect of a royal visit prompted the directors to authorise Aitchison to 'expend some money on decorations for the Prince and Princess's visit to Llanberis and to have an engine and carriage in readiness' when they met on 3 May 1902. The Prince of Wales, who was to be installed as chancellor of the Welsh University at Carnarvon on 8 May, stayed at Vaynol as a guest of the Assheton-Smiths. On 10 May the royal party travelled from Carnarvon to the Dinorwic quarries by road so, although the Prince and Princess would have passed Aitchison's decorations and the waiting train, they did not avail themselves of it. The *Times* report records, incidentally, how some members of the party 'proceeded to Llanberis by Mr Assheton-Smith's mineral railway, for which some special carriages had been provided.'

Aitchison, a volunteer in the Royal Welch Fusiliers, was called to undertake 28 days training during 1900. He was authorised to arrange cover for his absence with a Mr Clay, whose salary was to be increased in consequence.

He placed the issue of his salary before the directors on 15 November 1902, pointing out that the commission agreed five years previously had never produced the anticipated amount. He left the meeting with his salary increased to £500 free of income tax, backdated to 1 July and, apparently, the tax reimbursed by means of an expenses claim.

Judging by the lack of comment, Aitchison's position with the NWNGR gave the directors no cause for concern and when, on 9 January 1904, they were informed that he had been offered an appointment with the North Wales Power & Traction Company they approved it without demur. They even agreed to recruit a hotels manager to give Aitchison time for his new position, but required him to take a £70 reduction in salary as a consequence. Joseph P. Pullan was appointed to the hotels post by 12 March 1904; salary £150, plus 10% commission on net profits over £700.

NWPT, which was about to take over the parliamentary commitments of the Portmadoc, Beddgelert & South Snowdon Railway, had ambitious plans for developing both an electricity transmission network and electric railways connecting Portmadoc with Bettws y Coed, Corwen and Carnarvon via Beddgelert, the first link including the Croesor Tramway and the last the NWNGR. (Not relevant to the railway story, Pullan introduced some innovations to the hotels and left in 1908; reading between the lines, he had an 'interesting' private life that Aitchison and the directors did not know how to deal with. He was replaced by Miss Pryce Jones at the Victoria and Miss Bessie Timothy at the Padarn Villa.)

Receiving salaries from the NWNGR, NWPT and the PBSSR as well as SMTH, Aitchison was doing quite well for himself. On 16 February 1907, he informed the directors that as an agent for insurance companies he received the commission on the company's policies. In February 1910 the directors awarded him an honorarium of £50 for 1909 on account of the £70 he had relinquished when he took on the NWPT appointment and Pullan was appointed. On the death of his father-in-law in 1910 he resigned from SMTH to take over the family firm; he referred to his departure as retiring. His notice expired in October but the directors gave him paid leave until 30 November, thereby paying him until the end of the company's financial year. They also agreed to pay him £210 annually, plus expenses, to continue as the company's consulting engineer.

On 10 September 1910, the directors had no hesitation in accepting Aitchison's recommendation and appointing J. R. Owen to be his successor as 'secretary, traffic manager, superintendant of the line and works in charge of the railway and businesses other than hotel management.' His salary was to be £156, payable quarterly, much less than Aitchison was paid, even taking into account responsibility for the hotels being devolved to Miss Pryce Jones for a salary of £80. First working for the contractors, Owen had been with the company since 1895. When he married in 1907 the directors had subscribed

£4 for a present. Both Owen and Jones were instructed to maintain contact with Aitchison 'on all important matters'.

When £50 was set aside for distribution amongst the 'regular' employees on 3 February 1914, 'in recognition of their services with extra traffic', it was conditional on Owen having £20 of it, the remainder being divided as Aitchison and Owen thought best. On the same occasion the directors resolved to ask the shareholders, at the general meeting, to approve their own payment, £50 each and £70 for the chairman. Owen's salary had been increased by £25 from 17 February 1913 and a further £50 from 1 December 1915. It was increased to £400 on 12 July 1919.

On 14 January 1905, Aitchison had 'reported a temporary arrangement he had made with respect to office accommodation for the company who are taking over the working of the NWNG Company [NWPT] and asked for confirmation.' SMTH reserved the right to terminate the arrangement if it needed the premises. In February 1906, NWPT was given permission to route telephone wires on the SMTH poles, on a wayleave of 1s per pole, and to terminate at the office that it rented.

A request for wayleaves by the NWPT dealt with on 8 April 1905 might well have taken the form of Aitchison writing to himself. The directors agreed to allow the transmission route to cross ground near Dolbadarn Castle for £2 10s and across the tramroad between the waterfall and the river bridge for £5, each sum being paid annually.

There was an unspecified problem, probably unpaid rent, with the use made of SMTH facilities by PBSSR and NWPT during 1909. By 10 July the room had been vacated without notice being given and by 11 September Aitchison reported that the company had received payment in lieu. Aitchison was to make arrangements to take over the NWPT telephone.

As part of the hotel business SMTH inherited and operated a fleet of road carriages, including an omnibus. The latter had been declared 'unfit for use' in 1898 and Aitchison was authorised to replace it. On 5 September 1903, Aitchison was instructed to 'continue his inquiries this winter re motor cars and if possible to inspect the cars used by the Great Western Railway at Helston in Cornwall after they had been in service some time.' The GWR motor bus service between Helston and the Lizard had been started on 17 August 1903 and was the first regular road service run by a UK railway company. The company did not buy a motor bus. Although it had refused an offer to buy a charabanc from the Rycknield Engine Company on 9 September 1905 the company was in a position to sell one for £21 in 1911.

Below: **The up starting signal is prominent in this view of No 4 departing for the summit from Clogwyn.** *SMR*

Top: **The summit with the SMR on the right. The home signal and one of the starting signals stand out against the skyline, 1900.**
Valentine/Author's collection

Above: **Not too long after the line was opened, the wind has already beaten the summit station building's rendering into submission. The picture shows that the terminal tracks were not on the same gradient.**
Author's collection

As always with the arrival of a new technology there are those who want to find its limits. On 14 May 1904, the directors approved a request from Charles Jarrott and W. M. Letts 'to ascend the line in a motor car...' An earlier attempt by Harvey du Cros using a 15hp Ariel had been reported in the *Times* on 28 January; following the railway, it had failed owing to snow near the summit. Using a 5hp Oldsmobile driven by Letts on 6 June, the Jarrott-Letts attempt got within feet of the summit buildings in 61 minutes, 37 minutes without stops. The car was shadowed by a train and photographs of both together were taken at Clogwyn (p55). Du Cros had made a successful second attempt on 26 May, taking nearly four hours and experiencing several mechanical problems en route; his car was returned to Llanberis by train.

The impact, literally, of a different new technology was considered by the directors in 1916, Owen reporting that he had, acting on instructions, insured the company's property against aircraft risks on 6 May. The directors appeared to have second thoughts about the risk, for when the £36 policy became due for renewal it was cancelled.

The minutes contain several references to locomotive matters, although by no means supplying a comprehensive record of them. On 14 November 1903, Aitchison had been '

authorised to obtain what was necessary for repairs to engines and rolling stock and to keep the duplicate stock up to requirements', the first time rolling stock maintenance had been mentioned for four years. A year later, Aitchison 'was authorised to purchase the necessary repairing [sic] for the tramway and also to experiment with other tubes if found necessary.' It appears that there was no formal strategy for maintaining the stock. From 1903 a depreciation fund of £946 15s 7d had been maintained on the balance sheet without explanation, but presumably for railway assets as the auditor always noted that no allowance was made for depreciating the hotels' equipment.

Serious damage to locomotive No 4 was dealt with when the directors met on 11 July 1908. Aitchison was instructed to order a new firebox and tubes from the Hunslet Engine Company, Leeds, and to have them fitted. It might be reasonable to interpret this requirement as arising from an incident where the boiler water was allowed to run low, a situation that could have had serious and possibly fatal consequences. Another locomotive problem was manifest on 8 May 1909, when Aitchison was authorised to adopt a policy of ordering 'copper coated tubes when requiring any as it was considered that this might overcome the corrosion difficulty'

No 3 was the subject of attention on 11 September 1913, with Aitchison reporting that its outer firebox had a crack and was leaking. Although a repair in accordance with the insurance company's requirements was authorised, it was 3 February 1914 before an instruction was given to send it to Hunslet.

The only time a carriage came to the directors' attention was on 14 February 1911, when one of them was reported as requiring renovating and repairing; it was sent to the contractors' yard at Ince, near Wigan, for the work to be done. The lack of explanation leads to speculation that to need renovating when the remainder did not, the carriage concerned had been in an accident, and might possibly have been one of those derailed in 1896. However, it had been returned in June, when Aitchison saw it being tested and taken through the points at Hebron. Fitted with new wheels, its pinion did not mesh properly with the rack; he ordered the packing plates to be removed and the brake to be adjusted.

Share transfers approved on 10 September 1904 confirmed the position of the contractors as major shareholders in their own right, 591 shares being transferred to King and 441 to Holme.

In January 1912, the auditor pointed out that there had been nothing written off against the company's preliminary expenses and suggested reducing the amount by £1,292 2s 2d, leaving a balance of £1,000, appropriating the existing depreciation fund, £946 15s 7d, and £345 6s 7d from the profit and loss account for the purpose. He then suggested that there was sufficient credit in the profit and loss account to justify paying a 1% dividend to the shareholders, a recommendation the directors adopted. This dividend, and ½% paid for 1912, were to be the only returns the original shareholders received, unless they attended the AGM and took advantage of the train ride offered.

As the debentures approached maturity, the company bought back and cancelled several holdings: £700 in 1912 and £2,300 in 1913, the transactions making a capital loss of £1,179 for the investors, SMTH having paid 45% for £500 and 50% for the rest of the 1912 purchases, and 65% for £1,000 bought from Banner and £1,000 from Clegg's executors. In 1913 the investors' loss was applied to the depreciation fund and the remainder of the preliminary expenses, £1,000, were written off.

There were few changes to the SMHT board over the years and directors who resigned or died were not always replaced immediately. Cragg resigned in December 1906, Turner had died by 11 July 1908, and Clegg by 14 February 1910. King, Holme's partner as contractor, became a director from 11 May 1907 and W. Coltart Cross from June 1910. Holme died in 1912 and was replaced by his son, Clinton James Wilson Holme, from 9 September. King had died by 12 February 1917.

A fire at Halfway on 26 September 1910 destroyed the timber station building and its contents, including the telephone and the wiring to the staff instruments. The directors instructed that the railway's buildings should be insured and the cabin replaced by a brick building. Saunders recommended changing the instruments for automatic miniature instruments, but on 14 February 1911 the directors resolved that the instruments should be repaired by the Railway Signal Company. Arising from a report that Owen submitted about the fire in July 1911, he was authorised to obtain two extinguishers for the loco shed.

Two serious accidents, one a fatality, had been considered on 14 November 1910. Ben Roberts, a fireman, had been killed, presumably on duty, because there had been an insurance claim. The directors appeared only concerned to know why the insurance company had not paid the doctor's bill of £5 5s; it was settled by 13 May 1911. No report of the fatality has been found in the local press. The other incident had involved damage done to railway property by a trespasser walking to the summit at night to watch the sunrise; the chief constable was asked to take steps to protect the company's property. When the summit station was broken into on 1 July 1911 and damage 'estimated at about a sovereign' was done the matter was left to be dealt with at Owen's discretion if the culprits were traced.

The railway appears to have become something of a playground when the trains were not running. The *North Wales Chronicle* reported the case of William Morris Griffith, a quarryman from Groeslon, who was killed. On Sunday, 18 September 1910 he was walking down the mountain with friends having spent the night at the summit, when he decided to ride down the rack on a rock from a place below Clogwyn. Another rock was set off after him and hit him, knocking him off near Halfway. A witness said that Griffith turned over three times in the air before falling to earth; he died of his injuries the next day. At an inquest on 30 September the coroner returned a verdict of manslaughter against persons unknown. William Robert Jones, a draper's assistant of Pen'rallt, Carnarvon, appeared before magistrates to face the charge on 10 October and was committed for trial. Giving evidence for himself the following week, Jones admitted placing a stone on the rack,

saying that he removed it because it would not go more than two or three yards. Other witnesses said that several stones had been placed on the rack that morning. The jury found Jones not guilty, a decision greeted with 'vigorous applause'. No one admitted placing the stone that killed Griffith. Incidents of 'rack riding' are still spoken about by railway personnel.

'... the start of the European war had sadly affected the company's receipts ...' Owen reported on 2 September 1914. Revenue on the tramroad had been reduced by £805 10s 2d compared with 1913, the total reduction being £1,313 2s. Faced with having to raise £16,000 to redeem the debentures on 1 July 1915, the directors resolved to ask the holders to extend their investment for a further five years at 5% interest. Only four holders, representing £1,700, refused. SMTH's offer to redeem at 70% was also rejected although one holder was prepared to settle for 90% and another for 95%. Because of the requirement for all debenture holders to agree to the re-arrangement a meeting was held on 16 July.

The outcome was a resolution to extend the debentures until one year after the end of war, and that if any debenture holders disagreed a receiver was to be appointed, with a recommendation that Owen was to take that post if required. This time all the debenture holders agreed to the extension.

An unpaid bill of £6 15s by Wyman & Sons, the newsagents, for guides supplied in 1912/3 prompted SMTH to join the Liverpool Trade Protection Society in November 1914. Following the society's intervention the bill had been settled by 10 February 1915.

After a valuation of the SMTH's property was carried out to determine its liability for investment value duty in 1915, Aitchison's firm, Smith, Woolley & Wigram, was employed to check the Government's figures.

Owen reported an increase in traffic revenue when the directors met on 8 November 1915. He attributed a reduction in business at the summit to the lack of trains taking walkers to the area, saying: 'the bulk of the people who visited Llanberis were the better class, who made the journey by motors, and ascended the mountain by train, requiring little or no refreshment at the summit.' He also reported having increased the fares by 20%, to 6s adult return, during the two weeks that trains ran in October with the result that revenue had increased when compared with the same period in 1914. The fare increase, the first since 1896, was made permanent on 14 February 1916, when Owen was given discretion to reduce it if it was found to affect receipts.

No 4 at the summit terminus.
Pictorial Stationery Company/ Author's collection

Pickles, No 1's driver on 6 April 1896, had stayed with SMTH, becoming foreman driver. Owen reported on 14 February 1916 that he was 'in extremely failing health and that a good deal of time was lost by him.' Following his death on 26 September, Pickles was replaced by Sellars, another 1896 veteran, despite the instruction given to Owen when he reported Pickles' poor health 'to recruit another man to be trained up with a view to him taking charge of the locomotives when it became necessary.'

By this time the railway had almost certainly lost younger staff to the war. When Aitchison's call-up had been noted on 18 November 1914, the directors had agreed to keep his position open until he returned, and to pay him until 30 November. The 'plate-layer ganger's' departure was recorded in May 1917, from which time the work was carried out by casual labour. On 26 November 1917, Owen reported that the staff was much reduced and the men remaining had not only been in the company's employ for 18-20 years but were working for pre-war rates of pay. (Aitchison, incidentally, ended the war with the rank of Lieutenant-Colonel and did not resume his association with SMTH although he did return to work for the NWNGR.)

Increased travel restrictions affected traffic during the war, although Owen reported that train revenue in August 1916 had exceeded £1,200, £150 more than 1915. By November, however, limits on the use of petrol were responsible for a loss of £300 on the traffic. The fare increase had generated £375 in additional revenue, a 'considerable assistance' as expenses had been higher. Assuming the fare increase was applied pro rata, some crude arithmetic suggests that 7,500 passengers had been carried.

One expense that was not increased was that for maintaining the signalling system, Saunders' application for a 50% increase until the war ended being refused on 27 November 1916. Presumably in an attempt to attract revenue, on 12 February 1917 Owen was told to ascertain if the railway could be of service to the Government, but in September he reported that the War Office had rejected the offer. Seeking land for allotments, Llanberis Parish Council did not like the terms offered and complained to the landlord, the Vaynol Estate, which put pressure on the company to release the land on terms agreeable to the council.

An early Easter and lack of travel facilities in 1917 prompted a decision not to start operating until May. When the directors met on 26 May Owen explained that despite deferring the service until 21 May, there had been no passengers. The situation was hampered by the impossibility of displaying posters and printing guide books and handbills. In July, Owen reported that he had been unable to get the LNWR to agree to run more trains to Llanberis or to get the chief constable to agree to SMTH running a charabanc service from Llandudno. By November, the tramroad's revenue was reduced by £1,674 7s 8d compared with 1916.

The directors were despondent when they met on 18 February 1918. The company had a debit balance of £1,511 6s 11d on 1917's trading, little money in the bank, and they saw no hope of improvement while the war continued; 'the company was in a serious predicament.' Owen was instructed to consult the solicitors to establish the company's position with regard to its leases if it was put into voluntary liquidation, and to have the plant valued.

By 25 May, he had offers of £13,000 from Marple & Gillott Ltd of Sheffield for the railway and £8 per ton for the rails from Muirhead & Co. His conversation with a local bank manager had produced an offer from a Llandudno estate agent to act as agent for a sale on 4% commission. Owen suggested the directors should seek £24,000 for the railway alone or £26,000 for the railway and hotels.

Saunders & Company gave notice that they would terminate their agreement to maintain the signals and telegraphs when it expired on 30 June 1918. As it was unlikely that the staff instruments would be required, said Owen, he would endeavour to make other arrangements for the telephones to be worked for the present season, thus setting in train the situation whereby block working was abandoned.

Banner had produced a possible purchaser when the directors met on 9 July 1918. Sir Thomas Salter Pyne had been chief engineer to the Afghan government and responsible for introducing many industries to that country. He was told that he could have the ordinary shares for £1 each and the debentures for a sum that would produce 5% interest. Even though some effort was made, negotiations dragged out, and despite Pyne's office writing on 12 February 1919 that the sale would be completed within 10 days, on 12 July 1919 the directors, having learned that the securities that had been lodged to support the sale had been returned to their owners, gave up hope of it.

The possibility of a transfer of control, if not ownership, came from another direction later in the year. On 16 October 1919, Banner informed Owen by letter that he had been approached by Samuel G. Bibby, chairman of the Dolgarrog-based Aluminium Corporation, suggesting a share and debenture exchange between the companies; Owen was to research the corporation and its prospects. The suggestion seems a little bizarre, for the corporation was more than four times the size of SMTH by capital value so it could not have been a merger of equals. By the end of the month Banner was chasing Owen for information so that he could reply to Bibby, but on 9 December Banner told Owen that Bibby was considering making a cash offer. If details of these negotiations were given to the other directors it was not recorded in the minutes.

With no serious sign of a sale in view, the future of the locomotives, and the direction of the railway, was considered. As 1919 turned out to be the best year in the company's history, no doubt helped by a fare increase to 7s 6d approved on 12 July, the directors turned their attention to ensuring that the railway was fit to continue operating. On 13 October 1919, Owen was authorised to purchase new pinions and carrying wheels for the locomotives and carriages and in May 1920 shareholders were to be told that repairs to rolling stock and buildings were in hand 'and having failed, during the years of war to maintain in the best of order the repairs now on hand are extensive, and consequently will absorb a large proportion of the credit balance' of £2,770 7s.

Banner had responded on 20 October 1919 to Owen's regular report, referring to the section dealing with the locomotives and asking him to 'consider the question of applying electricity to the railway and merely putting the present engines into proper repair.' On 30 October he asked if the existing stock would need to be scrapped '... if we used electric engines, could we not use both? I see it done on the London railway lines.' The London & South Western Railway informed Owen that its own electrification schemes had cost £8,660 per mile including sub-stations. He also wrote to the Berner Oberland-bahnen. SLM quoted £33,000, including four 300hp overhead-wire locomotives at £6,000 each. The directors were to reject this as too expensive on 15 December 1919; any surplus funds, they decided, should be used to redeem debentures.

Meeting on 13 October 1919, the directors had thought that as the 'existing locomotives are getting old and may at any time give way' they should consider acquiring a new locomotive but had deferred a decision until Banner's opinion could be

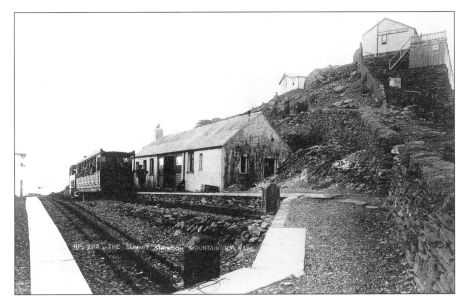

Left: **The summit station building was quite weathered when this photograph was taken. The summit hotel's verandah, upper right, has windows in its structure.**
Author's collection

Below: **The cover of a brochure produced by Jarrott & Letts promotes their successful attempt to drive a 5hp Oldsmobile to the summit in 1904 (p52).**
Judith Pettit Collection

obtained. The stock was more than 20 years old, there was insufficient room to store all the carriages under cover and none of it appears to have received a strip-down overhaul. It would be interesting to know if pinions had not been renewed before 1919, as today they are replaced after 18 months in service. The lack of heavy maintenance would have been taking its toll on service reliability for some time, not just during the war.

An order for spares: eight rack pinion wheels, 12 piston rings and four pairs of spindle glands, approved at the same meeting was placed with SLM on 4 November 1919. The forged pinion rings were sub-contracted to an English company and SLM hoped that a target price of £60 per ton would not be exceeded.

Owen returned to the topic of buying another locomotive when the directors met on 12 July 1920, saying '… four locomotives [are] on the road and … in case of a breakdown we [have] nothing to fall back on … owing to the increase in traffic and the fact of the charabancs arriving at Llanberis at about the same time the demand on all days, in all probability could not be met.' He should have offered some of the parties a discount to travel at a different time. Quotations were sought from Hunslet and SLM, the former writing on 4 September that it could not supply for at least 18 months and declining to tender. SLM submitted two quotations on 30 August: £5,700 for a loco as already supplied and £6,050 for a loco 'which offers important advantages in comparison with your existing type, for instance: double-armed rocking levers … instead of single-armed levers, and the engine working with superheated instead of saturated steam. A smooth run of the train results from the former and a considerable economy of fuel and water from the latter improvement.' After being told that the prices were high, on 1 October the company blamed the exchange rate and offered a credit note for the difference if it moved in SMTH's favour. On 1 November 1920, the directors decided that £5,700 was prohibitive; SLM had reduced it to £5,100 by 15 December.

With the need to renew rolling stock and redeem debentures the directors were quite willing to consider an offer to buy the Padarn Villa Hotel for £1,500 when they met on 16 February 1920. They responded with a counter-offer of £2,500, which was accepted by 15 May 1920; the furniture fetched £570 11s. Bessie Timothy, the manager with 13 years' service with the company, had lost her job with the sale. The directors gave her six months' salary in lieu of notice and permission to live at the Victoria Hotel during that period if she had not obtained another appointment. In 1906, the Padarn Villa lease had been extended, following which the company sold building plots on the site, the proceeds

seemingly being applied to revenue, rather than capital. The 1920 proceeds were applied to the depreciation fund.

Profits made in 1919 produced bonuses totalling £42 for the heads of the commercial departments and weekly bonuses of 17s each for the other employees on 16 February 1920. Owen's salary was increased to £500; on 15 May he also received a bonus of £100 in respect of 1919.

On 1 November 1920, the directors were informed that George Browne of the Silver Motors Company at Llandudno had been charged £50 to use the railway route to climb the mountain by car, an unusual commercial initiative, albeit not one that was repeated.

When bonuses for 1920, another record year according to the annual report, were considered on 21 March 1921 the four departmental heads received £27 between them and Owen received £200 free of income tax. Traffic got off to a rocky start in 1921 the directors were told on 21 May. The railway had opened at Easter and was then closed for a month owing to a coal miners' strike. When services resumed the locos burned timber until the coal supply was restored.

The prospect of a sale to Pyne had re-surfaced on 15 May 1920 when shares were transferred to his nominees: Harry Shaw (135), Betty Shaw (3,299) and James Douglas Moffat (428). Shaw was considered for nomination as a director but since there was some doubt about his eligibility legal advice was to be obtained. Despite additional transfers of small numbers of shares to Pyne nominees, the likelihood of him taking control came to an end with the transfer of the Shaws' holding of 3,583 shares to Sir John Henderson Stewart Bt on 21 March 1921.

With Henry Joseph Jack and Evan Robert Davies, Stewart was promoting the Welsh Highland Railway and in July 1921 he was to take control of the Festiniog Railway.

Stewart owned a distillery in Dundee and was said to have made money during the war; his baronetcy, for public services, was awarded in 1920 and may not have been unrelated to a £50,000 donation made to an unidentified political party. Davies was a solicitor from Pwllheli and life-long friend of the politician David Lloyd George; he had worked in George's personal office during the war. Jack was managing director of the Aluminium Corporation at Dolgarrog. Jack and Davies were both elected members of Carnarvonshire County Council.

In 1918, the corporation had taken over the North Wales Power & Traction Company, which owned the Portmadoc, Beddgelert & South Snowdon Railway, including the erstwhile Croesor Tramway, and in 1920 took control of the North Wales Narrow Gauge Railways.

Stewart had acquired the corporation's railway assets to enable them to be incorporated into the WHR in January 1921. At a time when the nation's main-line network was being amalgamated into four groups, the trio created their own group of narrow gauge railways. Whether Bibby's earlier approach had any connection with Stewart's acquisition of SMTH is unknown, as are the origins of his partnership with Davies and Jack. Whereas control of the FR was necessary to ensure the WHR's development, acquiring control of SMTH was most likely opportunistic, based on the fortuitous availability of Pyne's shares.

Stewart's SMR shareholding was reduced to just 38 shares on 21 May 1921. 25 shares were transferred to Jack, 25 to Davies and 3,500 to Branch Nominees Ltd, a subsidiary of the National Provincial Bank.

It is most likely that the shares registered to Branch Nominees were being held as security for loans obtained by Stewart for his own purposes. On 24 October 1921, 90 of these shares were transferred to nine persons, 10 each, including Gwilym Lloyd George, Walter Cradoc Davies, Davies's brother, and several employees of the corporation, and on 16 January 1922, the remainder, 3,410, were transferred back to Stewart.

SMTH's 1920 offer to redeem debentures at 70% had received a poor response, only £2,000 being redeemed at that rate. Another £600 was redeemed at 75%, including Fox's £400 holding acquired via a broker who received 2½% commission. In 1922, the company had a better response when it offered 90%, buying £3,600 from contractor King's daughter, £1,000 from Banner, and £3,500 from Holme.

With the price reduced to £3,500, on 24 October 1921, Owen was instructed to order a 'new steam rack locomotive of improved type' to be delivered in April 1922. SLM complained that it was forgoing its profit on the transaction. By 16 January 1922, the £2,000 deposit had been transferred into a joint account with the SLM. The £2,000 and interest would be paid to SLM when the loco's boiler had been tested, £800 when the loco was ready for shipping at Antwerp, and £700 six months after delivery 'as a guarantee of sound material, good workmanship and satisfactory working', together with 5% interest accruing from the date of shipping.

In an apparent act of rebellion by the outgoing directors, and not mentioned in the minutes, was a decision to honour the company's chairman from 1896 by giving the new locomotive his name. A respected accountant with experience in company reconstruction, Banner had been a member of Liverpool City Council from 1895 until 1912, Unionist MP for Everton since 1905, Lord Mayor of Liverpool in 1912 and was knighted in 1913. He was to be created a baronet in 1924, and died in 1927. His accountancy firm was to lose its independence after its part in the London & County Securities Bank Ltd's collapse in 1973 was subject to criticism.

Stewart's takeover of SMTH was well under way when the directors met on 18 March 1922, Banner announcing that he was negotiating with Jack and Davies to sell 'certain shares' for £3 each. By 27 March, Davies had agreed to buy 1,500 shares at that price, leading to his and Jack's election as directors subject to confirmation at the general meeting.

On 18 March, the directors had also dealt with bonuses for 1921, awarding £33 to the heads of departments and £100 to Owen, the last act of direction by the old regime.

Visitors enjoy the vista from the roof of the 1953 summit building in 1936. Protection was added later, see photographs on p73. *Valentine/ Author's collection*

5

Under new management

Stewart, Davies and Jack formally took control of SMTH at the general meeting on 6 May 1922. Banner, Holme and Cross received £350, probably £150 to Banner and £100 each to the others, as compensation for their loss of office.

The new regime's first board meeting had taken place on 12 April, when Jack and Davies had formally accepted Banner's resignation and elected Stewart a director and chairman. Despite his investment, Stewart was not to attend any board meetings.

Owen was instructed to pay all accounts by cheque where possible and to cash a cheque to pay the wages. He reported on the condition of the infrastructure and rolling stock and said that the new locomotive was delayed. He was to arrange maintenance of the company's lines, telephones and staff instruments and arrange for the GPO to install a telephone. The beneficiaries of share transfers included Jack (750) and Davies (763) with small holdings being retained by Holme (86) and Banner (195); the source or sources of the shares concerned were not recorded on this occasion. Davies reported that he had been in touch with the LNWR and Red Garage concerning combined bookings.

Courtesy of the 1921 Finance Act, Owen was able to report a refund of £606 16s 2d in overpaid passenger duty. Fares had also been exempted from the duty if they were less than the unspecified minimum ordinary fare.

Over the course of meetings held on 12 April and 6 May, Davies and Jack made fresh arrangements for souvenir sales on SMTH property. A decision not to let the bookstall out as previously was countered by an 'amended' offer of £40 from Mr Francis, its regular occupant. He was told that he could have the right to sell Goss-crested china for £40, but that the company would sell other gifts, including china, and that the company would review the arrangement at the end of the season and gave no pledge to renew it. Davies was to arrange for stocks of suitable goods to be sold at Llanberis and the summit, with two or three girls to be employed, dressed in Welsh costume, to sell them. Two girls were soon employed, but without the Welsh costumes. In 1934 Davies was to arrange for a schoolgirl in Welsh dress to act as stationmistress on the WHR.

An accident occurred on 9 June 1922 when a Mr Wade was injured. A train was at Clogwyn Coch when a casting broke and the loco 'shot forward'. The automatic brakes came into effect and the train stopped. The casting was attached to 'the' cylinder according to the *Carnarvon & Denbigh Herald* on 16 June. As in 1896, Wade had jumped out and hurt his leg.

Having surveyed the railway on 27 May and 5 June, Davies and Jack recorded their objectives for the business at a meeting held on 24 June 1922. Concerning the railway, one of the summit buildings was to be used as a tea room, another partly as a refreshment bar and partly as accommodation, and the third as a bookstall. A new concrete flat-roofed hotel on the station site was to provide covered railway accommodation, seating for 250, lounge, kitchen, 'sanitary conveniences', and bedrooms for 50 guests. Posts indicating the height above sea level were to be erected at half-mile intervals along the line; the existing lavatories at Llanberis were to be converted into a bookstall with new facilities be provided adjoining the old offices. The Llanberis refreshment room was to have French windows giving access to the platform, its balcony was to be modified to give access to both the platform and main road, and the riverside platform was to be extended and widened. Regarding rolling stock, prices for new locomotives and carriages were to be obtained. Owen was to develop afternoon excursions to increase late afternoon and evening traffic, 'even at reduced fares'. Davies was to organise the publication of a 'new book containing extracts from eminent authors dealing with the Snowdon district and illustrated' and to arrange for SMTH's insurance policies to expire 'at midsummer'.

It was to be more than 10 years before the summit got its new building and then it was much smaller than described.

Far left: **Evan R. Davies**

Left: **Henry Joseph Jack.**
Welsh Highland Railway Heritage Group

Snowdon and Welsh Highland Holiday Book   125

SWISS LOCOMOTIVE AND MACHINE WORKS
WINTERTHUR (SWITZERLAND)

British Representatives

Bernard Holland & Co.,
17 VICTORIA STREET, LONDON, S.W.1

Rack Locomotive supplied to the Snowdon Mountain Tramroad and Hotels Co., Ltd.

Suppliers of every kind of LOCOMOTIVES
"Winterthur" Gas and Diesel Engines, Crude Oil Engines, Rotary Air Compressors and Vacuum Pumps.

Experience of more than 50 years in
RACK LOCOMOTIVES
as a speciality

Boyd (see Bibliography) saw the remains of only one height post, at Waterfall, when he was surveying the line.

The business's fire insurances were itemised in detail. Of particular interest, with valuations, were the 'two small carriages' at £300 each; five large carriages, £600 each, and five locomotives, £1,500 each. The risk of damage arising from the use of steam boilers was covered up to £3,500 each. Third party cover put a limit of £20,000 of claims in any one year. Insurance for five locomotives informs us that No 6 *Sir Harmood* had been delivered by this date; its arrival was not otherwise recorded.

The stations were listed as station house, waiting room, dwelling room, store room, domestic offices, 'all under one roof or communicating known as Waterfall station', £300; Hebron and the summit station were similar, £300 each. Llanberis station comprised booking office, booking hall, waiting room, porter's room and lavatories, £500; furniture and fittings, £50; refreshment room, bar and store, £1,200; engine shed and fitters' workshop, £1,500; dwelling house, offices and store, £600; office furniture, fittings, books, stationery and instruments, £200, and store adjoining, £50. The house and store were stone-built with slate roofs, the other buildings being timber with slate roofs. Clogwyn signal cabin was brick-built with a corrugated iron roof, £50. Davies's legal practice arranged the insurance and took half of the commission.

Jack's ideas for timetables and increasing locomotive water capacity, to avoid having to take water en route, do not appear to have impressed Davies. The former were left for Owen to deal with and Jack volunteered to consult Fox regarding the latter.

The other issues dealt with on 24 June included the transfer of the registered office to Davies's office at 7 Victoria Street, London, and the appointment of William Richard Huson as secretary, a role he performed for the other railways in the Davies/Jack/Stewart empire. Owen was to continue as general manager without any reduction in salary.

A consequence of this change was that Owen ceased to attend the board meetings, and to write the minutes; after 1894 there had been only three meetings not recorded in his hand. Previously, the minutes had been mostly recording matters arising from Aitchison's and Owen's reports, but now they were to reflect the directors' concerns and there was, in consequence, less minutiae about operational matters recorded. Judging by the small amount of correspondence that survives, Owen and Banner had been in regular contact, writing several times a week.

Finally, on 24 June 1922, Davies reported a meeting that he had had in London on 22 June, with Fox and SLM representatives about new rolling stock with SLM quoting £3,750 for a new locomotive to be delivered in 1923. Discussing the need for additional safeguards, Fox had said that SMTH would be quite safe running carriages with a capacity greater than 60.

On 11 August 1922, Davies was requested to negotiate with SLM for two locos and a carriage. Davies and Jack, together with one of Fox's engineers, were to inspect Swiss mountain railways to decide on the best type of carriage, to determine the most effective method of increasing capacity, 'by providing more passing places or otherwise', and observing the latest developments in mountain railway practices and amenities. This visit might not have taken place, for on 27 August 1923, Davies alone was instructed to visit Switzerland with a similar brief. He must have departed straight after the meeting, for on 19 February 1924 he was to say that he had visited Switzerland 'last August and September'. In addition to being shown the SLM works he 'inspected and travelled upon' several railways and funiculars, noting that several lines ran trains of two or three carriages without problems. He was assured by SLM representatives that the SMTH's new locomotives were quite capable of 'taking a train of two coaches'. Experimental trains with two carriages were to be operated during 1924.

Railway wages were the topic of a meeting convened by Davies and Jack at Dolgarrog on 29 September 1923, Davies and Owen having discussed the issue at Llanberis the previous day. They considered a list of the personnel concerned, seven of whom were still being paid the bonus introduced in 1919. New rates, as listed, were introduced from 1 October, removing the bonus and paying a small increase over the basic rate. A train crew returning to Llanberis after 4.30pm would be paid an extra 2s 6d each.

Name	Duty	Wages	Bonus	Total	Proposed
John Sellars	Driver	£3 8s	17s	£4 5s	£3 10s
T. Williams	Driver	£3 3s	17s	£4	£3 5s
C. Parry	Driver	£3 3s	17s	£4	£3 5s
E. Roberts	Driver	£3 3s	17s	£4	£3 5s
R. Williams	New driver	£3	Nil	£3	£2 5s *
W. Thomas	New driver	£2 5s	Nil	£2 5s	£2 *
B. Griffiths	Fireman	£1 10s	Nil	£1 10s	£1 10s
John Hayes	Bailiff	£2 18s	17s	£3 15s	£3
H. Williams	Conductor	£2 13s	17s	£3 15s	£2 15s
E. Hughes	Conductor	£2 8s	17s	£3 5s	£2 10s
H. Jones	Conductor	£2 15s	Nil	£2 15s	£2 5s
O. Griffiths	Ganger	£2 18s	17s	£3 15s	£3
Mr W. Edwards	Stationmaster			£4	£3 10s

* for winter

There are some queries about this list. The bailiff, not mentioned elsewhere, was presumably the estate manager. The writer assumes that the ganger was employed full time and had the assistance of additional labour on a seasonal basis.

The order for two more locomotives, 'similar to the one last supplied and known as *Sir Harmood*', was sealed on 1 December 1922. The price was £3,500 each payable in four instalments by 1 October 1925, 5% interest being payable on the deferred payments. Reflecting Jack's concern, tank capacity was increased after the order had been placed, the additional cost of £24 per locomotive being approved on 12 January 1923. The existing rolling stock was reviewed on the same date, Davies and Jack agreeing to pay £25 for an SLM employee to overhaul and test it before it was put into service later in the year. There can be no doubt that the stock required qualified attention, but it must be doubtful that the time available was adequate.

Locomotive names were also considered on 12 January 1923, *Aylwin* and *Eryri*, being chosen for the new machines. No 6's tenure bearing the former chairman's name turned out to be brief, for the decision to rename it *Padarn* was recorded at the same time. An order for two replacement nameplates was placed with SLM on 23 January 1923 at a cost of £3.

Removal of rock at Llanberis to improve access to the yard and create more space for charabancs was underway in December 1922. The blasting risk was insured for £7 10s and the employer's liability at 7½% on wages estimated at £300.

Davies and Jack were considering improvements to more of the railway's infrastructure on 12 January 1923, reporting discussions with Ralph Freeman of the engineers now known as Sir Douglas Fox & Partners, on installing a second track from Llanberis station to a new loco shed and the provision of additional passing places. None of this work was done.

They were obviously confident about the ability of the business to fund these capital investments, and the new locomotives, without putting any special financial arrangements in place beyond a £7,000 overdraft from the London City & Midland Bank. This was increased to £9,000 by 27 August 1923.

Owen's proposal to reduce the fares 'in view of the general reduction of fares on railways and in view of the reduction in wages on this railway' was considered on 2 February 1923. The new adult fare was to be 8s, railway and charabanc companies paying 5s 6d before 8 July and after 15 September. In the summer the party fare of 6s would be available before 11am and after 3.30pm. The previous increase above 7s 6d had escaped recording.

A decision to 'negotiate for the purchase of a site for pleasure gardens at Aberglaslyn' had been reported on 11 August 1922. More details were given on 2 February 1923, when Davies said that the 100-acre site offered 'particular and exceptional advantages for laying out a pleasure park and tea gardens, possessing great natural beauty …' Located at the Nantmor end of the pass, the WHR would shortly run through it. He was authorised to negotiate up to a maximum price of £2,000. The likelihood of the Goat Hotel at Beddgelert being offered for sale shortly was also considered as it could be operated in conjunction with the Victoria Hotel and its value

SIS carriage No 9 loaded for transport to Wales, in August 1923. *SMR*

'would be greatly enhanced by the opening of the Welsh Highland Railway.' Jack was to negotiate to buy it, including fishing rights, and to bid at auction if necessary, for up to £6,000. An offer of that amount was made to buy the hotel as a going concern, but the vendor wanted £6,500.

The Aberglaslyn purchase was protracted, presumably because SMTH did not have the spare cash to pay for it. In December 1925, a three-year tenancy for part of the land was agreed with the Nantmor Copper Company Ltd despite the purchase being incomplete, SMTH offering to pay interest on the outstanding balance to the vendor. In an example of environmental concern, SMTH required the copper company to provide safeguards against polluting the river.

Expansion of the SMTH business in association with the group's railways progressed when Jack reported that he had proposed to the FR and WHR that SMTH should have exclusive rights to operate refreshment rooms and bookstalls on those lines at a rental of £50 for each. Agreement was reached, not surprisingly, and rent was paid from 1 August 1923. Bookstalls were provided at Blaenau Festiniog, Tan y Bwlch, Minffordd, Beddgelert and Snowdon and combined bookstalls and refreshment rooms at Portmadoc, Dinas and South Snowdon. The inclusion of Snowdon and South Snowdon, both names given to Rhyd Ddu on the WHR, in both lists may appear to be an error, but it was intended to provide two rooms for refreshments and one for the bookstall there. On 21 July 1925, the minutes record agreement to pay ground rent of 10s annually for the refreshment rooms at Blaenau Festiniog, Portmadoc, Beddgelert and Dinas.

The Blaenau Festiniog bookstall cost £85; Portmadoc New, £400; Beddgelert, £75 and Dinas, £375. The latter was partly on land leased from the LMS by the WHR for £1 per year. Tan y Bwlch bookstall building was transferred from Llanberis and a temporary refreshment room was provided at Minffordd.

The non-completion of the Aberglaslyn purchase by the time Davies and Jack met on 27 August 1923, and the 'other immediate obligations of the company', were given as the reasons for deferring the pleasure ground development until 1924.

Two carriages had been ordered from SLM by 14 April 1923, the maker having tendered £1,350 per vehicle. A price had been requested from the Metropolitan Carriage & Wagon Company, too, but that company had either declined to bid or its price was too high. SLM had given SMTH deferred terms again, a total of £2,621 to be paid by 1 October 1925. Sub-contracted to Société Industrielle Suisse (SIS) of Neuhausen, delivery was expected by 20 June 1923.

The new locomotives were despatched promptly, No 7 on 24 March and No 8 on 10 April; the delivery notes survive at Llanberis. Following inspection and testing by Swiss Federal Railways' engineers, they had been shipped via the LMS at Antwerp, the journey taking 18 days in the case of No 8. 'Erector' Ekhardt commissioned them for SLM.

An order for new carriage brakes, 'to provide additional safety', had also been placed by 14 April 1923, at £110 per vehicle, a total of £770. An SLM engineer was to commission the new locos and carriages and to fit the new brakes. It is not clear if this was in addition to the engineer who was going to overhaul the stock or instead. The carriages and brakes were not delivered as quickly as the locomotives, however. Due by 20 June, they had not arrived when Davies and Jack met on 27 August. The delay was due to 'certain difficulties ... by reason of negotiations between the Swiss company and Sir Douglas Fox & Partners ...' They were still awaited by 19 February 1924, when Jack and Davies considered a bill

submitted by SLM, agreeing to pay £500 in addition to £500 paid in December, and to pay the balance of £1,057 5s 3d on 1 July 1924.

SLM was now prepared to send a fitter to install and adjust the new brakes on the existing stock for £1 15s per day plus expenses. Herr Habegger was to spend five months in Llanberis from April 1924. The new carriage brakes took the form of an automatic overspeed device.

Fine tuning might have been required, as on 22 August 1924, when 'not far from the summit [the] engine and passenger coach parted company, and a few minutes later the coach crashed heavily into the locomotive. Passengers were

hurled against one another, though without more serious injury than a few bruises and a bleeding nose or two.' The report, from the *Manchester Guardian*, noted that a new automatic brake had recently been installed. Under the heading 'a slight mishap', the *Carnarvon & Denbigh Herald* quoted it in full and obtained a statement from the railway. The incident had actually demonstrated the efficiency of the braking systems, in that the carriage had stopped, and the collision had occurred after the brake had been released. Two or three passengers in the compartment nearest the loco had been alarmed, sustaining 'nothing more serious than a bump.' The statement concluded 'Since it was opened 26 years ago the Snowdon Railway has enjoyed almost complete immunity from accidents. A slight mishap occurred last year but that also went to show that, owing to the efficacy of the brakes, under no conceivable circumstances can the train get out of control.' No explanation was given for the locomotive and carriage separating sufficiently to activate the carriage brake. And in current times the statement's compiler would be sent on a course to learn how not to make a situation seem worse than it is.

In the directors' report for 1923, the shareholders were told that '... as the [carriages] were not available until the close of the season, they made no contribution to the earning capacity of the company.' The following year they were informed that 'Owing to the wet weather experienced during the summer, full benefit of

the two additional locomotives and coaches was not derived ...'

Davies obviously had a yen for publicity. By 2 February 1923 the new book that he had proposed on 24 June 1922 had evolved into the *Snowdon & Welsh Highland Holiday Book 1923*. A substantial number of advertisements had been received, worth £243 12s 6d by publication, and both the FR and WHR had agreed to pay £50 'in consideration of space and illustrations being devoted to the attractions of their railways and the district through which they pass', which would not have been too difficult in view of the positions that he and Jack held with those railways. A total of 20,000 copies were to be printed and W. H. Smith & Son, Wyman & Sons Ltd and other booksellers agreed to take copies.

There were regular reports of approaches that Davis had made to the main line railway companies and charabanc operators in pursuit of traffic. He had approached Thomas Cook & Sons, the Polytechnic Touring Association, the American Express Company and others to get them to promote seven-day inclusive holiday tours based on the Victoria Hotel; the holidaymakers would pay £8 8s per week and the tour companies would receive 10% agency commission.

Davies was also instrumental in arranging a visit by 30 journalists and railway officers to the area that started on Friday 22 June 1923. Departing from Paddington courtesy of the GWR, the party was routed via Blaenau Festiniog to the FR and

Top: **No 4 has a high level of draught exclusion in this view. The bricks in the wagon might date it to 1934-7, when the summit building was under construction.**
Author's collection

Middle: **With the signal pulled off, a train prepares to leave Llanberis. The man watching from the railings also features in a photograph taken at Beddgelert station on the Welsh Highland Railway in 1934/5, where he is pretending to check tickets. He is not one of the directors, but might he be the SMR's manager, Roberts?**
SMR

Below: **Four locos on shed, August 1927, of which Nos 2 and 5 can be identified.**
R. E. Tustin/Author's collection

Portmadoc, by the WHR to Beddgelert and by motor vehicles to Llanberis. The next day it travelled to Carnarvon and Dinas by motor vehicles and to Beddgelert on the WHR, the motor vehicles returning it to Llanberis via Waenfawr, viewing the Marconi radio station en route. After lunch the group travelled on the SMT. SMTH provided accommodation at the Victoria Hotel and other hotels in Llanberis. The lack of organised activity on the Sunday, before the LMS returned the party to London on Monday, serves as a reminder that there were no trains on Sundays, although evening entertainment was provided by the Llanberis Male Voice Choir on both Saturday *and* Sunday. Afterwards, Davies was to report that articles had appeared in 12 newspapers and a film had been shown in 1,200 cinemas.

During December 1923 there were several transfers involving Stewart's shares. At the beginning of the month he held 3,443 shares in his own name and 1,634 deposited with Branch Nominees. On 6 December, 3,410 of his shares were transferred to A. B. & M. Bank Nominees Ltd. By 13 December, 2,000 of these shares had been transferred back to Stewart and then to Jack. Similar transfers were being made with his FR shares at the same time. Seriously in debt, Stewart was to commit suicide on 6 February 1924. When Davies and Jack met on 19 February 1924 they not only recorded his death but also his resignation, dated 12 December, as a director. The transfer of the shares held by A. B. & M. Bank Nominees Ltd to Stewart and then to Jack and of Stewart's own holding to Jack was registered at the same time. The author cannot help but be sceptical about the propriety and timing of these transfers. Jack became the chairman.

On the company front, George Westall, a rating surveyor with connections to the North Wales Power Company (NWPC), was appointed a director on 1 April 1924, just 14 days after he had become a director of the FR Company, also a consequence of Stewart's death. Restructuring the company by increasing its share capital to £100,000, changing its name to Snowdon Mountain Railway Ltd, and revising the articles in relation to the directors and auditors was considered on 18 June 1924; a shareholders' meeting was to be called, but no action was taken.

Discussions with the Inland Revenue bore fruit in December 1924, when that organisation agreed not to assess SMTH as a railway for income tax purposes, saving £207 18s for the 1922/3 tax year. The revenue had also agreed to the written-down value of SMTH's plant and machinery being set at £23,091 and to depreciation being calculated at 4% of that amount. A claim for income tax and corporation profits tax of £1,951 19s 6d was to be settled for £1,200, payable in three monthly instalments from May 1927.

Capital expenditure 1922-28

	New locomotive cost and carriage	Additions	Additions, alterations and repairs
1922	£3,649 15s 2d		£2,813 6s 3d
1923		£12,839 16s 1d	£17,109 3s 6d
1924		£365 10s 1d	£6,001 17s 6d
1925		£385 11s 11d	£388 12s 6d
1926		£396 8s 9d	
1927		£1,577 19s 2d	
1928		£777 4s 11d	

With the objective of clearing the overdraft and funding capital investment, Jack had been charged with arranging a new debenture issue. On 19 February 1924, he reported negotiations with the Investment Registry, whereby £50,000 would be made available. IR would take £30,000 and the SMTH directors would place not more than £5,000, the balance to be issued when the company's requirements and revenue justified it. In the meantime, Jack had made a temporary loan of £4,000 at 8% against an agreement that no new debentures would be issued until the loan had been repaid. A Mr A. M. Williams had advanced £2,200 on the same terms; it was to be revealed that this money was also Jack's.

There was to be no debenture issue. By June 1924 the overdraft stood at £10,500 and before the end of the year the bank was calling for its elimination. This placed SMTH in a quandary. If it settled the overdraft it could not pay SLM money due in August 1925. Reaching a settlement with SLM to pay half the debt in August and the remainder in 1926 with interest, the overdraft was reduced to £6,427 4s 7d by October 1925. The bank then agreed to accept £427 4s 7d on 1 November 1925 followed by four monthly payments of £200 from 1 January 1926, subject to an undertaking not to create any charge on the

Right: **No 5 crosses the upper Afon Hwch Viaduct.** *Lilywhite/John Alsop collection*

Below: **No 8 has just passed Waterfall station returning to Llanberis. The SIS carriage has been repainted and lost its lining.** *Judith Pettit collection*

SMTH undertaking or property. Davies offered to 'find' the money to honour the undertaking if any loans he made were treated on the same terms as Jack's and Williams's – might he have borrowed money at, say, 5% to lend it to SMTH at 8%?

A year later the overdraft was down to £4,600 and was being reduced by £100 per month from 1 October 1926. SLM had been paid £728 14s 5d, leaving a balance at 8 October 1926 of £4,200 to be paid, plus 7% interest, in August 1927. Analysis of SMTH ledgers on 3 November 1927 had established that Jack had lent £21,137 11s (including the £2,200 lent via Williams) and Davies £3,055 0s 3d. The overdraft was then £3,200.

SLM had to wait even longer for its money. Still owed £4,200 in October 1926, by the time of a special directors' meeting held on 3 November 1927 it had agreed to reduce the outstanding debt to £2,200 and for it to remain outstanding

until the end of the 1928 season, subject to payment of 7% interest. A payment had probably been made in August 1927; the wording in the minutes suggests that some reduction had also been agreed.

These manoeuvres leave the impression of the directors running a financial juggling act and struggling to keep all the balls in the air. Sooner or later something would have to be done to introduce a measure of stability into the company's fiscal affairs.

Following the success of the holiday book published in 1923, several other publications appeared. Probably first published in 1924, as all seven locomotives are named, stocks of *The Book of Snowdon* were exhausted by December 1926 when another 2,000 copies were ordered from McCorquodale & Company. In 1925, the British Publishing Company had published an *Official Souvenir of the Snowdon & Welsh Highland Railways* at its own expense,

Left: **The track above Waterfall station. Hebron station is on the left of the telegraph pole, the summit peaks out on the skyline to the right, and Hebron chapel stands to the right below the summit.** *Lilywhite/Author's collection*

Below: **A 1920s snapshot, in this case at Hebron as a down train awaits the arrival of an up working; some of the passengers are obviously bored by the wait. The SIS carriage is still in its original livery and the signal shows signs of disrepair. If the signals had not been maintained since Saunders relinquished their contract in 1918 the weather would have been responsible for their deterioration moving progressively down the mountain.** *Andrew Thomas collection*

giving SMTH 2,500 copies for sale at 6d. When it was reprinted for the 1927 season SMTH paid £59 for 5,000 copies.

At the summit, one of the huts was found to have been severely damaged by storms on 1 January 1926. Two sides and the roof had been destroyed, the anthracite stove and its chimney had been dislodged and furniture scattered about. The Vaynol estate, concerned about the capital value of the license, refused to allow its demolition and replacement by a modified station building. The latter was sheltered and more accessible to those nervous about braving stronger winds to reach the huts. The Vaynol hut remained in use and the station building was adapted to serve refreshments in 1927. For 1928, the directors decided to provide five or six more beds for one of the huts and Owen

was instructed to run 'sunrise' trips in June and July, but not to increase costs in doing so.

SLM was consulted over the repair to a crack in one of No 7's cylinders in the autumn of 1926. The railway had asked how the piston valve sleeves could be removed, adding that it must have been faulty when manufactured. SLM explained that the liner had been pressed into the cylinder and that 'for removing same a pretty considerable effort is necessary.' A drawing was supplied, explaining how the liner could be removed. SLM also pointed out that No 7 had worked perfectly well when it was handed over after commissioning in 1924 and that any fault could not be one of manufacture. The builder went on to suggest that the damage was caused either by too little cooling water being applied during a descent or by cooling water being applied to a cylinder that was already overheated.

Being unable to repair the cylinder at Llanberis, it was sent to Switzerland, SLM adopting a puzzled tone when writing on 10 January 1927, carefully suggesting that the SMR was not being entirely truthful about the damage, pointing out that fresh machining marks were visible on the bush. The valve rods were not straight and the piston rings were not steam tight. The repair strategy proposed was presumably adopted. No other correspondence survives.

Davies's courting of the LMS paid off in 1927, when the directors attributed traffic levels remaining unaffected by the general strike, and the miners' strike that followed it, to the services provided by the main line railway.

There was an unexplained hiatus with the 1927 general meeting. Set for 27 December, it was postponed until 19 January 1928 and then until 16 February. It is notable that Jack was not present and was only represented by proxy on the last occasion; it may be that those attending on the first two dates held insufficient shares to form a quorum. In May 1927, Jack had stood down as the Aluminium Corporation's managing director, saying that he was on the verge of a nervous breakdown, and earlier in December he had intimated that he would not stand for re-election as a director of that company. Although he had dealt with SMTH matters during the year, most recently on 3 November, it may be that in December and January pressures were too much for him even to consider appointing a proxy to the SMTH meetings. With 4,143 shares, he was the largest shareholder. Surprisingly, Branch Nominees still held 1,648 shares, presumably the rump of Stewart's holding.

The 16 February meeting was followed by an extraordinary meeting that was the first stage in several changes made to stabilise the railway's position. The shareholders resolved to

Right: **The puff of steam from the air brake reveals that this photograph shows a descending train, in this case between Halfway and Hebron, *c*1933.**
George Woollam/Meg Davies collection

Below: **The guard looks on as his train is photographed while the locomotive takes water at Halfway.** *Author's collection*

divide the existing £10 shares into 10 £1 shares, to increase the capital to £100,000 by the creation of 30,000 7% cumulative £1 preference shares, and to rename the company the Snowdon Mountain Railway Ltd. The resolutions were confirmed on 1 March 1928. No explanation was given for the change of name but it did put the emphasis on the railway and suggests that no expansion of the hotel business was going to be considered. The decisions were found to be invalid, however, because the interval between the meetings was too short.

When the directors met on 28 March 1928, Jack proposed that Davies should become chairman when the change of name had been approved, Davies to be acting chairman in the meantime. He also suggested that Hubert Lander Westall, director Westall's son, an accountant, should take over from Huson as secretary.

The company had still not eliminated its overdraft or its indebtedness to SLM. In the case of the former, Davies reported that he obtained approval to overdraw an additional £250 until Whitsun, 27 May 1928, and to reduce the outstanding amount to £3,000 by 30 June and to £2,000 by September. With regard to SLM, the directors decided to ask if payment of £1,000 on account during the summer would be acceptable.

The Inland Revenue was also owed money and Davies had negotiated a settlement whereby £100 would be paid 'now',

followed three equal instalments in May, June and July, the current liability being met by two equal instalments in August and September. A demand for payment of £740 being considered on 6 November 1928, the directors resolved to offer £100 then, £100 in March 1929 and the balance in three equal instalments from July 1929.

The reconvened extraordinary meeting was held on 18 April and the resolutions were confirmed on 7 May 1928. The increase in capital was registered on 9 May and the change of name on 16 May 1928.

Following Jack's departure as chairman, he remained a director, several employees of the Aluminium Corporation or the NWPC disposed of their SMR shares; there is no way of telling, of course, if the events were related. On 24 October the directors resolved to buy 'three pieces of antique furniture ... a motor lawn mower, garden roller and two or three other articles' for the hotel from Jack, paying him £450.

As chairman, Davies took to contributing a report to the board, on 6 November 1928 reviewing the traffic in some depth. It had been better, 'not only in the sense that more money was taken but the undue crowding that had been experienced in previous years was largely avoided, because instead of relying upon the railways and charabancs as heretofore, there is increasing business every day from private cars which is distributed over the whole day.' As private motor-borne traffic would often travel in the afternoon when the weather had been off-putting in the morning, trains would be run at 5pm and 5.30pm in 1929.

Through bookings from the LMS had ceased during August because the train reached Llanberis 30 minutes later, about noon. After 23 September the through-booking fare had been reduced to 4s, from 5s, and charabanc operators had paid 6s to include lunch; the extra traffic had not justified the reduction and the 5s end-of-season fare would be applied in 1929. The use of canvassers shared with the LMS at Llandudno, Colwyn Bay and Rhyl 'worked very satisfactorily as regards Llandudno, a little better than last year at Colwyn Bay but [was] quite unsatisfactory at Rhyl.' Passengers from the latter were negligible, 'though large numbers of Rhyl passengers

Right: **Nos 6 and 8 at Clogwyn on 30 August 1926. The signals are still in place although the starter on the left has lost its finial.** *H. C. Casserley/ Publisher's collection*

Below: **By the time this train was photographed on the embankment above Clogwyn the loop had lost all of its signals.** *Excel Series/Author's collection*

passed through Llanberis daily in Messrs Brooks' charabancs.' SMR had shared a canvasser with the FR and WHR to work the resorts between Pwllheli and Aberystwyth in August and September; the GWR would not participate.

A car park attendant had been employed to control traffic in the station yard. Paid by tips until mid-August, he was then paid £1 per week plus one third of the takings above that amount. In 1929, he was paid £1 15s plus one third, generating £87 6s 6d profit for the company on a turnover of £151 16s 6d.

The requirement for visitors travelling to Llanberis by train or charabanc to return to their North Wales coast accommodation for their early evening meals was undoubtedly responsible for SMR traffic from these sources peaking around midday.

The newly formed Council for the Preservation of Rural Wales had made contact about the conditions at the summit. Following correspondence and meetings, 'the council expressed appreciation of the concern felt by the company as to the preservation of the amenities …'

At the summit a new refreshment room had made good profits. One of the huts had been repaired and would be provided with eight or ten sleeping berths before the 1929 season; supper, bed and breakfast and the rail ascent would be offered for £1 5s.

The problem of passengers taking space in the Llanberis refreshment room, only buying drinks to accompany their own food was considered. The woodland, now the car park, at the rear of the offices could be converted into a tea garden with facilities to serve hot drinks and light refreshments, where a charge could be levied on the seats occupied.

Discovering that the Lake District was visited by Americans, Davies had approached Atlantic liner companies, American tourist agents and the US minister of labor, a Welshman, to arrange for distribution of the company's literature in the USA. He had also made representations to the LMS to arrange excursions from Chester, a haunt of Americans, to Llanberis.

For the first time since Davies and Jack took over, gratuities were awarded to staff. Owen was the only railway employee so rewarded, with £20. At the hotel, Mrs C. E. Watson, manageress, received £20 and Miss Marion Thomson Jones, housekeeper, and Miss Elizabeth Jane Jones, assistant general, each received £5.

Despite having made a profit of £6,523 2s 6d and carrying forward £4,166 2s 11d after allowing for interest and tax in 1928, the company was still unable to meet its financial obligations. At the meeting held on 22 May 1929 the directors decided to try to defer the bank payment due that month until June. The Broughton & Plas Power Coal Company had written about its unpaid bills, and the secretary was to pay the February statement. The £220 due to William Hope & Sons at Caernarfon for boiler repairs was to be paid immediately.

The crunch came, though, when Jack had complained to Davies that not only had he been compelled to sell securities on a falling market to compensate for interest he had not been paid, he had been compelled to refuse several investment opportunities because his capital was committed to the SMR. He was not, therefore, willing to continue the loan on the present terms. The directors' immediate response was to pay the interest due from 1 January 1929 free of income tax but that was only a sticking plaster solution. By 1 December, the overdraft had been reduced to £1,700 and the SLM debt to £854.

Director George Westall died by July 1930 and his place on the board was taken by his son, the secretary, the appointment being confirmed at the general meeting held on 2 September

Top: **An atmospheric view of trains at Clogwyn, *c*1933.** *Irene Evans/ Meg Davies collection*

Below: **Looking towards the north west, No 5 climbs towards the summit. The can being carried on the carriage's buffer probably contains drinking water.** *Publisher's collection*

Bottom: **A train climbing towards the summit, *c*1933. Llanberis Lake is visible through the haze in the right-hand background and on the left of the train Llyn Fynnon y Gwas is partially framed by the smoke.** *J. Cook/ Meg Davies collection*

The Train on Snowdon. 9574.

1930. A further change in the share structure was approved on 30 September 1931, when the general meeting gave the directors permission to divide the £1 shares into four 5s shares. There were no board meetings between the 30 September 1931 and 29 September 1932, both dates being those of the general meetings. The Branch Nominees shareholding was acquired by Jack and registered to him on 6 December 1932.

Davies's 9 June 1933 report told about a poster of Llanberis Lake and Snowdon by Orlando Greenwood produced by the LMS. 5,000 copies were printed at a cost of £150, the SMR contributing £50 over two years. The LMS passed the original painting to the hotel on loan later in the year.

Under the heading 'general scheme of decoration', on 28 July 1933 Davies described recent works carried out to improve the company's property. 'The railings and the wood and iron work of the station and neighbouring buildings have been painted green and cream. Four of the coaches have been painted red, grey, green and orange and attract considerable attention. A red line has been introduced into the painting of the locos. The summit buildings have also been painted and the refreshment room at the terminus made more attractive.' At the same time, complaints had been received about 'the lack of adequate sanitation at the summit.' A water tank was erected there to collect rain water to flush the urinals and water closets. In 1934 Davies was to have

the FR and WHR carriages painted different colours, too, 'to develop the holiday spirit'. None of them was orange.

A way out of the financial juggling act was reported by Davies on 18 August 1933. With the aid of a stockbroker, he had negotiated a £30,000 5½% loan from the Prudential Assurance Company. To be secured by a first mortgage debenture, it would be repayable over 30 years by 60 equal half-year payments of £1,026 12s. The lender would have a first charge on the railway and hotel and a floating charge on the other assets. A 100-guinea arrangement fee was payable and the broker was paid 1% commission on the loan for his trouble. The Prudential had the option of having the company's insurance business.

The sum borrowed was actually £32,000, repayable in half-yearly instalments of £1,095 0s 10d over 30 years. Completed on 22 November 1933, legal costs totalled £800, of which £480 was paid to Evan Davies & Company. The money was used to redeem the outstanding 1895 4½% debentures (£2,900) and Davies's and Jack's loans (£26,011 11s 10d). The Aberglaslyn land purchase had been completed for a total of £2,300 in October, the vendor having agreed to forego his claim for interest, a move of some generosity considering it had taken some 10 years for him to be paid.

The eventual settlement with SLM was not recorded, but the relationship was sound enough for an enquiry to be made about

69

a new locomotive. The locomotive builder wrote on 2 October 1933 that an engine the same as the last three supplied would cost SFr66,000 instead of SFr 88,100 because material and labour costs had gone down. However, the exchange rate was against the SMR so that in Sterling it would cost £4,151 instead of £3,520. Construction would take up to six months from the date of the 'esteemed' order.

The directors treated the loan as a depreciation reserve and on 21 March 1934 told shareholders that the balance of any profits could therefore be distributed to them; on 3 May they agreed to pay a 5% dividend for 1933. Railway staff also benefited, their wages being 'restored to the level as at October 1931', subject to them working to a roster prepared by the manager, and to a review on 30 September.

At an extraordinary meeting held on 29 December 1933, the £1 shares were formally divided into four 5s shares and authority to create 7% cumulative preference £1 shares was modified in favour of 6% non-cumulative shares. The shareholders also agreed various items with a book value of £3,032 being written off.

A new building at the summit was first mentioned on 8 February 1934, when Davies reported that it, the installation of electric lighting at the hotel, and draining and levelling the Aberglaslyn land would cost approximately £5,000. He was therefore arranging to borrow another £3,000 from the Prudential on the same terms as previously obtained. There was no recorded debate on the need for a new building but perhaps the impetus for it stemmed from the previously noted complaints about the facilities there. What was not recorded either, was that the building's architect was Clough Williams-Ellis, proprietor and developer of Portmeirion, the Italianate village near Portmadoc.

On 16 February the *Manchester Guardian* announced that the building would be equipped with 'tearooms, tea-terraces and cloakrooms'. It would be 'a flat-roofed, modern building made of reinforced concrete and glass specially designed to withstand severe frost.' Williams-Ellis's chief architectural assistant said that it was designed to 'obliterate the present "blot" on Snowdon'. Williams-Ellis sent an item about the building to the paper that was published on 23 February 1934. The walls 'will be largely of glass, because of the view', the flat roof, which will form a terrace, will be of reinforced hollow tiles covered with asphalt. The lower deck comprises station hall, cloakrooms, lavatories, large restaurant, kitchens, services; the upper deck will contain sleeping cabins. The following week he told the *Carnarvon & Denbigh Herald* that the railway 'is becoming increasingly popular' and the 'existing agglomeration of timber and corrugated iron hutments ... are inadequate ... as well as dilapidated ...' The new building would

Top: **Walter Cradoc Davies.**
Gillian Davies collection

Above: **A train arrives at the summit station in 1933. When the tracks were repositioned to accommodate the 1935 building the station ground frame on the left of the picture was replaced by a two-lever frame on the opposite side of the track.** *Jack D. Colman/Meg Davies collection*

Right: **Ancient and modern at the summit on 30 August 1926. No 3 starts its descent whilst passengers disembark from a train propelled one of the 'new' locomotives. This is the only pre-war photograph of two trains at the summit seen by the author.**
H. C. Casserley/Publisher's collection

concentrate the facilities on one site and the station and restaurant should be in service during the summer, although 'it may well be another year before the further accommodation is added that will permit of the removal of the existing buildings ...'

Williams-Ellis went on to explain that the building 'is a frankly modern, functionalist erection, designed to do its necessary job in the most convenient and economical fashion ...' As if rehearsing arguments that were to be made 70 years later, he continued 'It might be argued by some that if a building has to be put up in such a place it should assimilate itself to the mountain by being built with Cyclopean blocks of the native stone. My own feeling, however, is that quite apart from the prohibitive cost ... and the fact that the mountain top would have to be quarried and despoiled to yield the stone, any attempted competition with its background in the way of mass or ruggedness would be rather futile.' Quite what he would think of stone being imported from Blaenau Ffestiniog and Portugal as used on the 2009 building can only be imagined.

Davies told the *North Wales Chronicle*, published on 2 March 1934, that it was hoped to devise a scheme to light the building by electricity and that it was anticipated that it would be finished by June or July. On 1 June 1934, however, the paper was to report that heavy snow had delayed the start of work until the previous week.

On 2 March 1934, the directors had agreed to let the contract to Messrs Gregory of Caernarfon on the basis of cost plus 10%. Good progress was being made, Davies reported on 21 August 1934, and he had 'hopes' that the building would be completed by the end of September. If no unforeseen difficulty arose, the directors resolved, an additional refreshment kiosk would be built 'at the end of the lavatory buildings.' The roof was 'nearing completion' on 2 October, when it was proposed to leave the final coating until the spring. Shutters were to be fitted to the windows. Some of the steelwork had been prepared at the Festiniog Railway's Boston Lodge Works. The building was located on the site of the original station building and the terminal tracks in front of it, making the railway slightly shorter.

Owen's 'continued illness' was considered on 2 March 1934. A doctor's report commissioned by Davies said that it would be in Owen's interest to be relieved of responsibility. Davies had also identified a temporary replacement, a David H. Roberts, formerly assistant district manager with the GWR at Chester according to the minutes. In 1938 Roberts, then aged 71, was to tell the *Liverpool Daily Post* that he had had 'nearly 50 years service with the LNER in Liverpool, Manchester and elsewhere'. He was to be paid £6 per week from the second week in March until the end of September and have meals provided by the hotel. Owen's 'lamentable' death, on 20 April, was recorded on 26 April. He had worked for the railway since 1894. Davies had attended the funeral and written a letter of condolence to Owen's widow. Roberts' temporary position became permanent from 1 May 1934 with a salary of £250 plus £50 expenses.

Another long-serving employee, John Sellars, No 2's driver in 1896, left the company during 1934, apparently of his own volition. He had become responsible for locomotive maintenance and on 25 July 1934, after he had left, Davies said

that he had been satisfied with Sellars' performance. A locomotive requiring 'a special repair under rush conditions' had been sent to the Port Dinorwic Dry Dock Company, a subsidiary of the Dinorwic quarry, however. The directors resolved not only to employ a new fitter but also to make greater use of the Port Dinorwic facilities 'in connection with the repair and overhaul of the company's engines.' Davies's careful choice of words and his tribute to Sellars indicate that there might have been a connection between the latter's departure and the locomotive in need of 'a special repair'.

When the loco had reached Port Dinorwic it 'had proved to be in a very unsatisfactory condition' and required a new boiler. Approving the expenditure on 21 August 1934, the directors resolved that the rolling stock should be kept in perfect condition and to accept the Prudential's offer to inspect the stock annually at a cost of £2 2s for each locomotive and £1 1s per carriage.

Another of Davies's ventures was approved on 21 August 1934. He had started a Welsh woollen department at Llanberis and had arranged to rent premises at 60c Guildford Street, off Russell Square, London WC, for nine months from 29 September to promote it. An advertisement for 'superfine Welsh woollens', with the address 'Department T, Snowdon Railway, Llanberis' appeared in the *Times* on 15 September. Nothing more was said of it.

The year 1934 was one of change for the directors. Jack changed his name to Henry Jack Macinnes; his co-directors were notified on 6 April. On 2 March, he had transferred 137,720 shares to Davies. On 25 July the latter was awarded a salary of £400 for his services as managing director, although he saw little of it, for he died on 2 December. Davies family oral history has it that he had been given a clean bill of health by his doctor the day before. Earlier in the year he had arranged for the FR to take a lease on the WHR and it may be that with the effort involved in running the three railways, legal practices in London and Pwllheli and as a politician, he had overreached himself. His eldest son, Cynan Evan Davies, also a solicitor, took his place as managing director and Macinnes resumed as chairman.

The minutes covering the period from the end of 1934 until 1940 are missing, but some insights into the company's activities have been extracted from the annual reports. Capital expenditure amounting to £131 3s 11d in 1936 was unexplained, as was £30 compensation received from the county council the same year and placed to the capital account. Also in 1936, a locomotive renewal fund of £500 per annum was established. Dividends were paid at 5% each year.

Only the ground floor of the summit building had been completed, at a cost of £3,791 9s 3d, when it had been brought into use on 19 July 1935. Expenditure was ended in 1937, when £6,158 9s 11d had been spent; beyond recording the expenditure, the directors did not deem it necessary to give the shareholders any information about the building. A photograph too poor to be reproduced shows scaffolding on the building when it had been taken on 7 August 1937, and a report in the *Liverpool Daily Post* on 2 July 1938 stated that 'the addition of sleeping quarters for staff and guests … are being put into commission for the first time this season'.

The continued presence of the huts during 1935 had prompted a reader of the *Times* to recall his experience of staying in one in the 1890s; it 'was not very pleasant.' In November 1937, Williams-Ellis, writing as chairman of the Council for the Preservation of Rural Wales, told the *Times'* readers that they had gone when he had visited the previous week. Without identifying himself as its architect, he observed that the new building 'has been placed on a ledge well below the summit and has been so designed as to be as inconspicuous as

Top: **In this view of No 5 descending the mountain the summit building has been completed and the cairn slightly reduced in height.** *Commercial postcard/ Author's collection*

Left: **The new building seen from the station side.** *Commercial postcard/ Author's collection*

Below: **In this 1938 view of the station, the crews of Nos 2 and 5 and a group of passengers pose for the camera.** *Valentine/Author's collection*

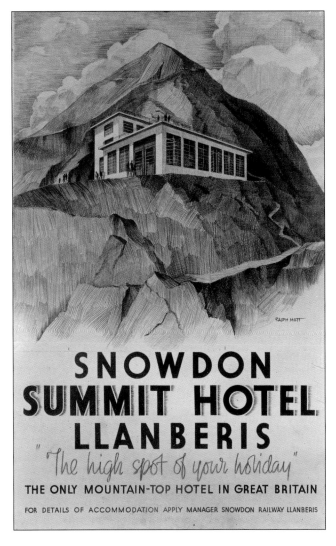

SNOWDON
SUMMIT HOTEL
LLANBERIS
"The high spot of your holiday"
THE ONLY MOUNTAIN-TOP HOTEL IN GREAT BRITAIN
FOR DETAILS OF ACCOMMODATION APPLY MANAGER SNOWDON RAILWAY LLANBERIS

One of two posters commissioned by the SMR from Ralph Mott to promote the completion of the 1935 building. The other poster is illustrated on p126. *Meg Davies collection*

may be.' Not quite the same as what he had told the *Carnarvon & Denbigh Herald* in 1934.

The operation of four trains on 21 July 1935, the first time the SMR had opened on a Sunday, met with opposition from the Llanberis Free Churches Council. '… a step forward to transform the seventh day into just another week day.' Roberts, interviewed by the *Carnarvon & Denbigh Herald*, explained that it was not for financial reasons but because of pressure from would-be patrons from England and South Wales. Some had driven from 'Manchester, Birmingham, Coventry and other large cities' for the weekend and had been disappointed to find no trains running on the Sunday. One visitor had told him: '… It is not such a terrible sin to ascend the mountain and see God's creation.' Asked if Llanberis residents had travelled, he answered: 'If we depended on the people of Llanberis, we would have to close within a week. We get no support from Llanberis, and 95% of those who went up last Sunday came by private cars, the remainder coming by rail from Carnarvon.'

During 1935, one of the drivers was a recently retired ex-LNER man from Wrexham, M. Edwards. On 11 July, the Gorton district loco superintendent wrote to ask for a certificate and enclosed £1 postal order to be passed on to him. On 20 August 1934, Edwards had been driving the 10.35am from Seacombe to Wrexham when he managed to prevent his train from colliding with a tree that had fallen across the line between Cefn y bedd and Caergwrle.

The opening of the summit building's accommodation in 1938 was reported in the *Liverpool Daily Post* and the *Manchester Guardian* on 2 July. 'The concrete building is a comfortable hotel…' There were seven bedrooms accommodating eight guests and a lounge with an open fire and a wireless. One of the bedrooms was larger and had a wash basin. Others had a divan bed, an iron bedstead or bunks. No tariff describing the differences has been found. There was central heating and lighting was provided by bottled gas. Drinking water was delivered in 'special cans.' A drying room was also provided. The building was managed by Liverpudlian Charles Gibson and his wife; they had worked on the mountain for four years, originally living in one of the huts. Gibson would get up early to see if there was any prospect of seeing the sun rise before waking the guests.

Photographs show that between 1935 and 1938 the refreshment room's counter was extended and oil lighting installed. The later photographs show roof-support columns, not visible in the 1935 photograph, attractively clad in timber. They also reveal problems with the flat roof, with clear signs of water ingress visible. This might account for public access to the roof being terminated soon after the building was completed.

The SMR's Aberglaslyn enterprise had been concluded with the property's sale to the National Trust in 1935. The land had cost £2,300 and £212 11s 1d had been spent on the car park but the whole was written down to £1,450 in the 1934 balance sheet; not a very productive exercise. How much the SMR received for is not known; the National Trust was given a donation to make the purchase. The *Manchester Guardian* demonstrated the media's traditional lack of understanding for railway matters by claiming that 'the land … will be purchased from the Snowdon Mountain Railway Ltd (whose line goes through the gorge here in a tunnel) …'

The outbreak of war in September 1939 found the railway having to deal with very different circumstances and, in comparison with the first, it was much more affected by it. Closure of the railway, summit hotel, bookstalls and refreshments was advertised in the *Manchester Guardian* on 5 September. The Victoria Hotel was expected to remain open but it, and the Llanberis bookstall and refreshment room, was immediately requisitioned for military use, although they were to be handed back on 16 December.

Initially, railway staff was kept on at the normal reduced winter levels and hours. Then, on 5 January 1940 the company introduced a five-day week as an economy measure.

In 1940, the train service was started at Easter and was moderately successful until a government veto was placed on holidays. In June, a cash flow forecast produced a deficiency of £45 by the end of July so arrangements were made to reduce staffing levels by 50%, partially by not replacing those who had left for other work. The Prudential loan payment due on 22 May was deferred, by agreement, until 30 September, 5% interest being payable until it was paid.

Prospects were so poor in May 1941 that the directors decided a train service would not be viable. The summit hotel was to be opened from 31 May as a trial, however. Roberts had resigned on 30 April (his wife had been ill), and Westall stood down as secretary owing to his own ill-health, and despite remaining a director he probably attended no more meetings. Ninian Rhys Davies, E. R. Davies's second son, was appointed assistant secretary from 1 June. Necaco Ltd, a company 'engaged on work of national importance in Llanberis', operating an observation post on Derwlwyn, was given permission to run a telephone wire from Llanberis to Hebron on the SMR route on payment of 1s per annum per stay, pole or bracket used.

Revenue from the summit during June, £162 4s 2d, exceeded that of the same month in 1940 (£107 3s 2d). The demand for a train service was such that the directors decided to re-open the railway for two months from 14 July, re-employing Roberts to manage it. With the employment of another driver or fireman, staffing was sufficient for two trains to be run daily and, for the first time, it would be a seven-day service. With revenue exceeding £900 by 6 September, the directors decided to keep the service running until 29 September.

Another contribution to the war effort was agreed on 10 September 1941. The SMR's lathe and drilling machine were to be hired to the Britannia Foundry in Portmadoc at an annual rental of £40, backdated to 1 September. This arrangement seems to have lasted for about a year. Reviewing the situation later in the month, the company had £1,280 in the bank, was entitled to an income tax refund in the order of £600, and awaited receipt of £700 compensation and rent from the War Department. Railway employees to be kept on during the winter were: Robert John Williams (clerk in charge); Evan Roberts (driver); Thomas Hughes (platelayer), and W. C. Jones (gardener). Consideration of payment to Prudential was deferred until May 1942.

The refreshment room and bookstall were requisitioned again from 29 September 1941, occupation being taken by the Air Ministry. Advance notice was given when the summit hotel was required for three weeks of experimental wireless work by the wireless regional office in April and May 1942. Exclusive use was granted for £10 per week with one train per week charged at £5, or two for £7 10s.

Considering the circumstances, a surprising amount of loco work was approved on 31 March 1942. No 7 was to be given a complete mechanical overhaul and Nos 5 and 8 were to be re-tubed; the Board of Trade had approved the steel for the latter. One of No 7's driving wheels had also been sent away to be re-tyred. Nos 3, 4, 5 and 6 were to be laid-up and the insurances relating to them cancelled. The railway would be re-opened at Whitsun, 24 May, providing Roberts would return to manage it. The employees were: Robert John Williams (clerk in charge); Evan Roberts (engine shed foreman and driver); Thomas Hughes (platelayer); Hugh Jones (fireman and platelayer's assistant), and John Owen (fireman and platelayer). They were given a 'small' pay rise.

The train service, daily except on Sundays, was operated from 23 May 1942 until 27 September. Writing on 23 September, the *Manchester Guardian's* North Wales correspondent reported that there had been two round-trips per day, a third of the normal number. The amount of coal consumed on each trip was 8cwt.

The Air Ministry also requisitioned the summit hotel from 29 September 1942 and on 2 October 1942 John Williamson, the FR's engineer, was commissioned to inspect the railway and report on it. Following a three-day inspection he submitted his report on 23 October. Generally, the track was in poor condition. Before the war 'a ganger and four men, and a boy for rack-lubricating, were fully engaged during the summer months.' Now the track was neglected and rough. The drainage gullys were silted up and did not serve their function, affecting the sleepers, 200 of which required replacing. The rack had not been lubricated for two years and showed signs of friction and wear. Much of the track was out of alignment. All the fishplates were rusted in place. The points were badly worn and required replacing. The embankments were suffering from erosion such that sleeper-ends were unsupported.

Williamson also commented on the method of train working. 'All the safety appliances have been dismantled and removed … the traffic … is now passed along the line by telephone control and what seems locally known as the 'interval' system; I have no knowledge of such working and if the telephones fail it must be a serious position. I have never heard of any authority who would give permission for such working, where two or more passenger trains would occupy the same section at the same time and I personally would refuse to permit the same without written consent of some controlling authority.'

He added a handwritten footnote expressing the view that the railway would deteriorate more rapidly if it was closed and that it would be better to run a skeleton service, but that such a service could not be run indefinitely.

Meeting on 21 December 1942, the directors were concerned about the effect of the Air Ministry occupation of the summit hotel. The ministry's contractors had started 'substantial' alterations and the railway had been run exclusively for its benefit. Now, with the works incomplete the project appeared to have been abandoned without notice being given. The directors did not comment on Williamson's report and obtained an itemised one from a Thomas Barratt to include the rolling stock. Abt had submitted a report on the track in 1936, of which only the title page survives; assuming that there were some, its recommendations appear to have been disregarded.

The requisition was terminated on 8 January 1943, leaving the company to claim compensation to restore the building. In addition to £1,467 5s 4d expenses incurred, including £400 for improving the track, the company sought £500 as a fee for the use of its facilities. No details were recorded about the changes made to the building, but they were enough to affect the railway's license to sell alcohol

Seen from the station roof, a train with carriage No 6 arrives. Since the building was completed the indefinite article has been added to the sign (p73). *Salmon/ Author's collection*

and needed to be undone. The Treasury solicitor was not impressed to learn that when Davies claimed his expenses for dealing with the requisition, he said that he should be paid both for work done as secretary and as solicitor.

Westall's death on 28 February 1942 was recorded on 28 July. Macinnes acquired 1,400 shares from his estate and transferred them to his (Macinnes's) wife, Charlotte Pauline. She and Walter Cradoc Davies, E. R. Davies's brother, were appointed directors. A total of 6,000 shares held jointly by the Davies brothers, inherited from their father, were divided between them in December 1942 and Ninian Davies became secretary from 1 January 1943.

Several changes to the company's office arrangements were agreed on 18 February 1943. The payment made to C. E. Davies as managing director was ceased, to be replaced by an annual fee of £250 paid to Evan Davies & Company. In return, SMR would have access to the facilities required by the Davies brothers to exercise their functions of managing director and secretary. Of this payment, £50 would cover the services of an accountant. The Davies brothers could also claim expenses incurred when travelling on the company's business. As chairman, Macinnes was to be paid £250, back dated to 6 April 1942, presumably to compensate him for the £250 previously paid for allowing his London office to be used as the company's registered office.

A comprehensive set of minutes was typed up for a meeting in 1943, but the date was left blank; approval to re-open the summit hotel on 31 May points to it being held, or intended to be held, earlier in that month.

Transcribed into this minute, Ninian Davies had written to Macinnes on 12 April 1943. There were 40 tons of coal in stock, Billingtons would supply 30 tons before the end of April and Broughton & Plas Colliery in Wrexham would contract to supply 100 tons at 20 tons per month: in all, enough to operate a similar service to 1942. He had met Williamson and inspected the track, on foot, with Hughes, the platelayer, and Williams, the clerk. There were 100 sleepers in stock, but he was trying to obtain more, and a gang comprising Hughes, Hugh Jones, John Owen and John Morgan would install them. A greaser would also be employed. Jones might have to work as a fireman when trains were run. The remainder of the train crew were Evan Roberts (driver) and Robert John Williams (conductor). The last time sleepers had been purchased, in 1933, they had cost £1 1s each; new ones would cost £2 5s.

There were four locomotives available for service, subject to boiler work being carried out on two of them by Port Dinorwic personnel. Williamson would supervise the operation for two days a week at the same rate paid to Roberts for full time. This was expensive, 'but Williamson is not in need, is 72, retired with a good pension and … points out he will have to pay away in tax half whatever we pay him.' Williams would be in charge in Williamson's absence. 'I have every confidence in him and after all, right through the winter he had sole charge of the running for the Air Ministry and managed it all without a hitch, and we ran five to six trains a day.'

Subject to track maintenance continuing, Williamson thought that a limited passenger service could be operated. Davies proposed a service using a single train leaving Llanberis at 1.15pm and 4pm to avoid using the loops, and the worn turn-outs.

From 1942 until 1945 the army used live ammunition during training exercises in the mountains. Although the exercises were not held near the railway an indemnity was obtained from the War Department and appropriate notices were posted in the booking hall and on the trains.

There were no more meetings until 5 June 1946, when W. C. Davies and C. E. Davies met to deal with the aftermath of Macinnes's death on 2 January, aged 77. His executors, his widow and Herbert Aubrey Crowe, transferred 15,000 shares to the latter. On 7 August, Macinnes's widow acquired 4,800

A pre-war aerial view of the summit. The groundworks that accommodated the original buildings are clearly defined.
Commercial postcard/Gillian Davies collection

SNOWDON, THE SUMMIT.

	1939	1940	1941	1942	1943	1944	1945	1946
Operating profit	£7,441	£350	£1,826	£2,305	£2,322	£1,622	£7,348	£5,929
Rents receivable	£91	£408	£175	£1,285	£1,282	£1,599	£1,009	£520
Interest on arrears of debenture interest			£105	£154	£193	£154	£238	£265
Creditors	£3,564	£3,684	£4,817	£6,627	£6,716	£8,038	£11,737	£11,548
Profit (Loss)	£4,955	(£1,881)	£338	£1,503	£1,500	£1,411	£3,457	£3,667

shares from five individuals and 111,580 from the estate, giving her control of £29,095 of the issued capital. Crowe, Macinnes's solicitor, had been articled to Evan Davies & Company.

An ordinary meeting was held on 16 December 1946, when the accounts for 1942-5 were approved. The delay in presenting the accounts was because 'the company's premises were under requisition from 1940 by various service authorities and ... the railway itself was run for various service and government departments for a considerable period ...' All claims for compensation had either been settled or were in course of negotiation. The railway had been re-opened to normal traffic in 1945 and the Victoria Hotel was re-opened at Easter 1946.

As a company, the SMR emerged from the war quite well, albeit at the expense of getting into arrears with the Prudential and of not paying some bills.

The first full directors' meeting since 1943 was held on 16 December 1946. The directors appeared to be much more confident about the company's prospects than their predecessors were in 1918. C. E. Davies was elected chairman and became managing director. T. G. Jack had been appointed locomotive superintendent after 1935 and had been called-up in 1939; he had returned to work on 15 November 1945, but got another job and left on 30 April 1946. Williamson had resigned as from 30 September 1946 and P. H. Jackson, formerly of the Southern Railway was appointed engineer and general manager from 17 December 1946; his salary was £600. Williams, the clerk, was designated assistant manager.

Compensation of £150 was received for 12 acres of land at Ddol Isaf that the Gwyrfai Rural District Council wanted for housing. Leased from the Vaynol estate, the land had been sub-let for agricultural purposes.

The arrears due to the Prudential at 22 November 1946 amounted to £4,865 17s 3d, increased from £3,185 12s on 31 December 1942, and the outstanding balance was £30,323 15s 7d. Taking into account the tax due on the interest, arrangements had been made to capitalise the arrears by increasing the amount covered by the debentures to £33,000. With six-monthly payments of £1,370 10s 10d the debt would be cleared on 22 November 1966.

On the railway, new points had been purchased and were being installed. An import licence had been obtained for new pinions ordered from SLM for delivery in June 1947 and orders had been placed for new bogie and carrier wheels. A licence had been obtained for timber with which to build a new carriage body. 'This latter work would be carried out as hitherto with direct labour,' the first reference to work being undertaken on the carriages. Eventually all of the stock was fully enclosed, with droplights fitted in the doors.

Meeting on 10 October 1947, staff conditions received the directors' attention. At a cost of £12 per week to the company, wages had been increased to bring them in to line with rates paid elsewhere in the locality. The permanent staff would henceforth receive 14 days paid holiday, seven days to be taken at the end of the summer season and seven days at Christmas. An outing was to be arranged for the permanent staff; this became a regular event, but the destinations were not recorded. Two long-serving employees, Evan Roberts (driver) and Humphrey Williams (conductor) had been awarded pensions of 10s per week on the understanding that if they were re-employed by the company the pension would be suspended; both had more than 30 years service. These enhancements had been arranged by C. E. Davies.

Despite not being a statutory railway, the SMR had issued privilege rate (quarter-fare) tickets to employees of main-line railway companies, 511 in 1947. Such tickets were conditional of the holders not seeking compensation in the event of death or injury following an accident. The National Union of Railwaymen had negotiated for them to be brought into line with other tickets and the Railway Clearing House had notified the company of the change. The directors decided that the SMR should not change its conditions.

Jackson, the new engineer, had estimated that it would cost £6,000 a mile to relay the line. Both he and C. E. Davies wanted a second opinion from SLM, and expenditure of £100 for this purpose was agreed. C. E. Davies was to investigate the provision

of a siding at Waterfall, to see if it would improve traffic flexibility, and the scope for improving the water supply at Halfway.

The gross takings to 8 October 1947 being £8,000 higher than in 1946, the directors decided to pay an interim dividend of 2½% at the same time as the 2½% dividend already agreed for 1946.

During 1948, 'abnormal' repairs were carried out on the locomotives, using £300 taken from the £500 rolling stock repair fund created in 1947. The repairs followed a visit from SLM's Herr Habegger; he was to return to 're-assemble two locomotives and adjust others' in May 1949. Also set aside was £2,203 18s 9d for repairs to the summit building, of which £75 6s 9d was spent in 1948. The arrival platform was to be cleared and reinstated before the 1949 season. In 1950, a quote for £4,500 was received for putting the building into a sound condition, the building's flat roofs being a particular problem.

For the first time in 50 years the railway came to the attention of officialdom. In June 1949 a Mr Jenkyns wrote to the Board of Trade from Llandudno: 'I wonder if you are aware of the general condition of the rails and joint-plates on the Snowdon Mountain Railway.' He went on to say that the original signals, interlocking and electric staff system had been scrapped 'without your authority, I believe' and 'the trains are sent up and down sometimes closely behind each other without any block working and the regulation speed of 4mph is often up to 9mph …' Claiming that there had been several derailments in 1948, he suggested someone be sent to conduct an incognito inspection. Neither the board nor the Ministry of Transport knew which of them, if any, was responsible and it took a while to track down the 19th century file because it had been deposited with the Public Record Office.

The ministry took the initiative and wrote to the company with a transcript of the letter on 28 September 1949, C. E. Davies replying on 24 October. He explained that the track had been examined by someone from SLM in 1947, 1948 and 1949. Following the first inspection the directors had decided to relay part of the line but it took until April 1948 to obtain the necessary licences. Some 2,200 sleepers were ordered from Robert Hudson & Company of Leeds and 4,320 yards of rail from Guest, Keen & Baldwins Ltd. The rail was delivered in August 1948, but Hudson could not deliver the sleepers. As soon as delivery of the sleepers had started, the relaying would start.

So far as the signals were concerned, they had been dispensed with c1921. Until then the company owned and operated four locomotives. Then three more locomotives were acquired and the then manager 'saw fit to dispense with this system, presumably on the grounds that it was not suited to the traffic on the line having regard for the low operating speed.' The traffic was afterwards controlled by telephone. His comment: 'I am given to understand that block signalling system has been discontinued on the majority of single lines in this country' attracted the marginal comment 'NO!!'.

The automatic brake being effective at speeds over 5mph and the journey time of an hour for just under five miles combined to refute the claim that trains ran as fast as 9mph. He denied that there had been any derailments in 1948 and described the

Norman Ronald Aubrey Crowe.
David Crowe collection

company's inspection and testing procedures. He concluded by mentioning the timetable, normally 30-minute intervals but 'if a more frequent service is called for, an interval of five minutes between trains is maintained.' The ministry merely acknowledged Davies's explanation and took no further action.

Charlotte Macinnes had died on 16 July 1949, aged 58; she had not attended a board meeting since 10 October 1947. N. R. Davies was to tell the author that he bought Jack's shares but such a transfer was not recorded in the minutes. By 25 September 1952 her holding was registered to Norman Ronald Aubrey Crowe and Monica Constance Mylne, her executors. On that date 15,000 shares were transferred to Crowe and Herbert William Bartlett, jointly, as trustees for David Edward Aubrey Crowe, Crowe's son, as a bequest. The remainder, 102,780 shares, was retained by Crowe and Mylne. It is probable that Davies acquired these shares after 1960. Reverting to 1949, Crowe and N. R. Davies had been elected directors on 29 November.

Towards the end of 1950 the directors had got the measure of Jackson, the engineer, and decided that as he preferred to spend time in his office rather than supervise the permanent way gang or produce the schedules of work required of him, he should be dismissed. He was given one month's notice that terminated on 31 December and two months' salary. On 1 January 1951 Williams took over as manager on a salary of £500, the board looking for a consultant engineer.

Another letter was sent to the Ministry of Transport on 10 October 1950. A Charles Allen of Brixham had written to complain about his wife's experience when she had travelled on the railway on 27 September. The circumstances had been almost the same as those in 1898 when the Reverend Adler had complained and it was almost exactly 52 years later. On this occasion Mrs Allen had travelled with a coach party. Despite poor weather the train had reached the summit and returned to Clogwyn without difficulty. There, on a ledge with a 2,000ft drop, said Allen, the gale force wind blew through the windows on one side of the carriage and, meeting the resistance of closed curtains on the other side, lifted it 'momentarily' off the rails. The few passengers on an up train transferred to the down and the ensemble returned to Llanberis without further delay or alarm. Allen claimed that the ticket seller had been heard to say that the conditions were so bad that he would not 'go up that day for all the money in the world.' If that was the case, asked Allen, why weren't the passengers warned? Someone had put these lives at risk, he said, and passenger safety should be the company's priority, not its revenue. He concluded that he had consulted the clerk to the Brixham Urban District Council before writing.

Once again, the ministry copied the letter to the company, C. E. Davies replying on 24 October 1950. Three trains had been run on 27 September, at 10.10am, 11am and 3pm. Mrs Allen travelled on the first. The only untoward occurrence was an obstruction blown on to the track at Clogwyn which was removed. There is no drop there and the 'lifting' sensation was caused by the carriage moving on its springs. After the passengers from the 11am had been transferred to the 10.10am both trains had returned to Llanberis. As to the remark alleged to have been made by the ticket seller, at that time the conditions were favourable, as confirmed by the Mr Allen's description of the ascent, so there was no reason for anyone to make such a comment. Davies concluded by taking exception to the claim that revenue took precedence over safety. No trains were taken higher than conditions permitted and refunds were given if conditions prevented a journey being completed. A copy of the reply was passed to Allen and nothing more was said.

Since the war, railway employees had started to join the Transport & General Workers Union, a transfer of allegiance from the NUR that some of them had joined in 1934. The organiser successfully negotiated a pay rise, recorded on 20 December 1950: shed foreman, £6 5s; drivers, £6; driver/firemen, £5 10s; platelayers, £5; firemen, £5; foremen platelayers, £5 5s, and carpenters, £5 15s.

A new boiler was approved on 14 November 1950. The last new boiler had cost £650 in 1936. Although the new one would cost £1,800, the 'expenditure would be justified in that it would give a seventh locomotive available for service during the height of the season and the revenue which the locomotive would earn would recoup … to no small extent the cost of the boiler.'

Although nothing more had been said about the complaints made about the railway to the Ministry of Transport, the ministry had not forgotten it. On 30 March 1951, an officer wrote to C. E. Davies reminding him of the previous exchanges and continuing: '… it did not appear necessary to pursue the matter further at the moment, but it is felt that it might be desirable for an inspecting officer of railways to take an opportunity in the near future of inspecting the line under actual working conditions … While it is appreciated that the minister does not have the same statutory responsibility for safety with regard to this line … it is considered that such an inspection would not only be of interest to this department but that the interchange of views thus afforded would be useful to all concerned.'

Replying on 2 April, Davies answered that he would he pleased to arrange for an inspection, suggesting that it should wait until the weather had improved. On 29 May, James Briggs, an engineer recently retired from British Railways' London Midland Region and newly recruited to the SMR, suggested that an inspector should accompany him during one of his visits to the railway.

Colonel R. J. Walker eventually made his inspection on 13 September 1951. He wrote to Davies on 21 September 1951 that 'In general, I found it well run and well maintained.' The track, allowing for its age, was reasonably sound but reaching the stage where major renewal was required, particularly the points, most of the new rails and sleepers obtained in 1948/9 had not been installed. He was concerned about the railway's system of block working by telephone; telephones were unreliable and messages could be misunderstood, especially if transmitted to drivers by seasonal staff. He thought that a better system should be employed and would advise if required.

A combined telephone and ticket system was devised based on military practice, where a paper ticket authorised the train movement through a section. Special arrangements covered the first train of the day, where the stations were unmanned until it reached them, and for running relief trains, where a second followed the first at a five-minute interval. Davies was closely involved in drafting the rules and producing the tickets and was obviously anxious to introduce the new system at Easter 1952, a target that was achieved. The rules were printed after the first season's experience did not reveal any shortcomings.

Coincidentally, the telephone cable from Halfway to the summit was found to be deficient in 1950. The purchase of 4,400 yards of cable from Pirelli, costing £646 16s, had been approved on 18 July 1951.

Faced with mounting losses on the Victoria Hotel since the war, £13,000 was to be quoted in 1951, during 1950 the directors had decided to sell it. The 16 years remaining on the lease being considered a hindrance to finding a buyer, an option to extend it by 21 years had been obtained from the Vaynol estate. Even then, hotel agents Christie & Company had failed to interest anyone in it. That company's representative visited the hotel in 1951 and thought that it was too big for the locality and could not be run profitably unless the rates were increased considerably. The directors decided not to re-open it in 1952.

At the summit, meanwhile, a programme of works proposed reducing the window openings and replacing the roof stanchions resting on the concrete floor with longer members that rested on solid ground. The works were carried out during 1952 using the deferred repairs reserve, the £795 0s 7d compensation for the damage done by the Air Ministry during the war.

The situation regarding the Victoria Hotel changed very quickly and it was sold to a J. Kushner on 31 December 1951. No value was attached to the lease and the furniture and contents were sold for £750, which sum was passed to the Prudential. The capital loss of £4,550 15s 8d was charged to the general reserve fund.

So, more than 50 years after starting in the hotel business and 23 years after company's name had been changed, the business included no hotels. Not recorded, it seems that accommodation facilities at the summit were not reinstated after the war. Because there was no breakdown in the published accounts there is no way of telling the impact of the hotel on the business. The Victoria Hotel benefited from considerable revenue investment over the years, improved plumbing, furnishings and electric lighting are three examples, whereas the railway suffered from the lack of it. The agent's comment about the rates suggest both that it had accommodated the cheaper end of the market and therefore that investment had been made without any effort to increase returns from it. In the report for 1951, the directors said of the disposal that 'the wisdom … should become apparent in the accounts for 1952 and succeeding years.'

The SMR as represented on one of Gallagher Ltd's 'trains of the world' series of cigarette cards. It shows No 7 painted black and one of the SIS carriages. The artist has not understood the locomotive's wheel arrangement. *Gallagher Ltd/Author's collection*

SNOWDON MOUNTAIN RAILWAY

6

The Post-war years,
changes in ownership and expansion

The SMR directors met rarely in the early 1950s, and then mostly to register share transfers. Consequently the minutes contain even less information about the railway's operation than was previously the case. On 28 July 1953, they agreed a rearrangement of the company's administration. Since 1943 Evan Davies & Company had provided management facilities for £250 a year, increased to £350 from January 1951. C. E. Davies had been paid a salary of £600 for his services as managing director and N. R. Davies had been paid £400 for his services as secretary. Under the new arrangement, backdated to 1 April 1953, the Davies brothers ceased to be paid their salaries and Evan Davies & Company was paid £1,700 for the provision of accommodation and services, including those of the Davies brothers as managing director and secretary. The author suspects that there was an income tax benefit in the revised arrangement. All of the directors were paid £100 annually for their services as directors, an arrangement that had started after Macinnes's death.

The crash of an RAF aircraft on 'the mountain railway line' on 12 August 1952, killing its three occupants, brought attention to the railway. Some 120 passengers were stranded at the summit overnight. After the track had been cleared trains were run to return them to Llanberis.

In 1954, the BBC paid £300 for the use of facilities at the summit. On the engineer's recommendation, approval was given to obtain sufficient materials to relay 100 yards of track annually, and an order was placed with Robert Hudson & Company. In 1955, the principal fare was increased to 12s 6d and in 1956 to 15s.

Staff requests for a £1 a week pay rise in February 1954 were countered by an offer of 15s, which was accepted. A year later, a deputation met Williams and asked for another £1 a week and for an extra week's paid holiday, the latter to compensate for working on three bank holidays. C. E. Davies, as chairman, thought that the pay rise was unjustified and that three days' extra holiday should be granted. Another £1 per week request in 1957 was negotiated to 4d per hour for a 44 hour week. Williams received a pay rise of £100 from 1 January 1956; he had been paid £550 per annum since 1 January 1952. An increase of £300 to the payment made to Evan Davies & Company, to £2,000, was backdated to 1 January 1956.

A locomotive crisis arose in 1956, with five boilers requiring substantial repairs following adverse inspection reports. To give breathing space whilst the problems were resolved the railway did not open until Whitsun, 21 May.

Above: **This photograph may date to 1956/7 but could easily have been taken before the war. The lining is the same as seen on No 2 in 1942 (Appendix 2), but the use of this livery before the war is not recorded.** *H. Thompson/Author's collection*

Right: **Llanberis on 10 October 1953. Carriage No 2 has been rebuilt but the doors remain unglazed. The kiosk accommodating the train controller was probably a consequence of the introduction of the train control system from Easter 1952.** *R. E. Vincent/ Publisher's collection*

SNOWDON RAILWAY TRAIN AT LLANBERIS W 5970

The period from Easter was usually fallow the directors thought, and the closure would not only save money on fuel and some staffing costs but would also make time for shed and permanent way staff to carry out further works that could not be carried out when the railway was operating. When the directors met on 5 April, the boilers of Nos 3 and 8 were at Hunslet and C. E. Davies and Williams were to visit to have the work advanced. No 5's boiler was to be sent to Hunslet with the objective of having the loco returned to service as soon as possible.

By July the first three boilers had been repaired at a cost of £1,300 each for Nos 3 and 5 and £2,500 for No 8. The boilers of Nos 6 and 7, sent to Port Dinorwic to have their fireboxes removed for examination, needed the same repairs as No 8, at a cost of £2,500 each, plus £450 each for new copper fireboxes. They were repaired in time for the 1957 season. When the order for the last boiler was approved on 15 October 1956 it was noted in the minutes that six locos would be available for service in 1957. The missing loco was No 4, having apparently been out

of use since c1938, but had been considered for 'rehabilitation' in September 1955. By deduction, the loco that received the new boiler in 1950 was No 2 (p79).

No account of the problem or expenditure, which cleared out the £2,000 locomotive replacement reserve, was given to the shareholders. Their 1956 dividend was reduced to 3% as a consequence, though.

Another expense in 1956 had been the £600 purchase of Mrs Williams's Vauxhall Wyvern saloon car, approved on 13 March. It was to remain in Williams's custody and control and used by him on the company's business. The registration was to be transferred to the company and the company was to be responsible for its licence and insurance. It was depreciated at £120 a year until 1959; from 1960 the entry in the profit and loss account became 'motor cars' and the amount varied, suggesting an increase in the fleet.

A rating assessment of more than £3,500 had caused some concern when levied in 1957. Seeking advice, a settlement was

Above: **Passengers board the newly enclosed No 7 in 1955 while one of the Lancaster carriages is on blocks in the alfresco carriage workshop to receive attention.** *Valentine/Author's collection*

Left: **The activities on No 7's footplate come under scrutiny in the early 1950s. The carriage has been partially glazed, as has the vehicle slightly obscured by the loco. The vehicle behind the tourist is in original condition. The passenger profiled in the window is smoking.**
P. B. Whitehouse

reached reducing the claim to £1,000. As a result the report for 1956 was not issued until June 1958 and those for 1957 and 1958 in July 1959.

The 1950s and '60s were good years for the railway and its shareholders. After the 1956 crisis had been resolved the four original locomotives were sent to Hunslet to be overhauled, No 2 in 1958, No 5 in 1959, No 3 in 1960 and No 4 in 1963. All seven locomotives were recorded as being in service in 1964, the first time this had happened for some time. No 4 was to be sent to Hunslet again in 1978, although it is not known why it needed major works so soon.

Financially, the company earned interest on money kept in a deposit account from 1957, and the Prudential loan was paid off on 21 November 1966. Before that had happened, however, on

9 November 1965 the company had obtained a seven-year mortgage from Gwyrfai Rural District Council for £3,090. Its purpose unknown, it was secured on a house called Aylwin, in Capel Goch Road, Llanberis. Dividends were paid every year from 1946 (2½%), peaking at 8% in 1959 and 1960 and then rising to 12% from 1961.

Andrew Owen Evan Davies, N. R. Davies's son, was co-opted to the board on 10 April 1962. A solicitor specialising in ecclesiastical law, he was to be installed as the diocesan registrar of the Canterbury Diocese in 1982. His uncle, Cynan Evan Davies died on 9 November 1963. In the annual report, N. R. Davies acknowledged his brother's service as managing director for nearly 30 years, saying that he had 'rendered devoted service' to the company and 'laid the foundation for its present prosperity'.

Above: **The SMR provided facilities for a live BBC TV broadcast from the mountain on 2 June 1956. One of the Lancaster carriages became a mobile equipment room and a mobile generator was loaded into the surviving four-wheeled wagon. The latter still has its brake. The loco, No 3, has its smokebox door painted silver.** *SMR*

Right: **A clearer view of No 3 when it was raising steam on the coal road on 24 August 1956. A set of shearlegs has been erected near the carriage being rebuilt.** *Author's collection*

He was replaced by his son, Morys Lloyd Davies, on 4 November 1963 and N. R. Davies became both chairman and managing director. On 31 December 1963 Williams, the manger, was co-opted to the board.

Gillian Davies, N. R. Davies's daughter, became a director in 1972; unlike her board colleagues, all solicitors, she was, and is, a barrister specialising in intellectual property law. Morys Davies resigned on 26 November 1976 to be replaced by Claude Francis Jackson from 1 January 1978. N. R. Davies and A. O. E. Davies had become joint managing directors in 1977. Gweneth Elizabeth Davies, the wife of N. R. Davies, was appointed to the board on 1 January 1979. Two outsiders became directors on 30 December 1981: William Ronald Whelan, a bullion and numismatic dealer, and Nicholas Peter Evelyn, a marketing executive. In 1976, 10 members of the Davies family held 166,051 shares, 59% of the issued capital. Jackson had replaced Williams as manager in 1970. The latter had ceased to be a director when the 1980 report was prepared; born in 1900, he had truly risen through the ranks in the company's employment.

Antony Armstrong-Jones, who married Princess Margaret on 6 May 1960, was almost a local man. Plas Dinas, the Armstrong-Jones's family home, is close to the Welsh Highland Railway station at Dinas. The creation of his title, Earl of Snowdon, on 6 October 1961 prompted the company to mark the occasion by presenting him with a gold medal that entitled him and his heirs to free travel on the railway in perpetuity. The

The 'truck', the works wagon, as it first appeared, looks as though the caboose was a section of one of the SIS carriages, approaches Hebron. *SMR*

medal was delivered to him at Kensington Palace by N. R. Davies. Many years later, following the publicity that surrounded the project to build a new summit building, railway personnel were surprised one weekend when Lord Snowdon arrived at Llanberis unannounced, presented his medal and exercised his right to travel.

The appointment of Ralph Sadler as consultant civil engineer in 1963 proved to be very successful. His recommendations enabled the SMR to overcome some longstanding civil engineering problems, including the regular flooding of some sections and the poor water supplies at Halfway and Clogwyn. No 7 was renamed after him following his death in 1977.

While the SMR was making civil engineering progress under Sadler's guidance, it made mechanical engineering progress under Claude Jackson's guidance. His appointment as general manager in 1970 brought with it a new element of experience and discipline. N. R. Davies was particularly complimentary to the author about his contribution to the SMR's wellbeing.

The railway's operation was not all smooth running, however. In 1973, immediately after the bank holiday on August 27, the line above Clogwyn was closed in order that it could be relaid,

	1972	1973	1974	1975	1976	1977	1978	1979	1980	1981	1982
Turnover £		246,349	291,134	384,530	442,849	478,522	554,827	541,128	584,864	612,488	
Overdraft £	8,107	8,222	22,406	29,259	23,877	34,392	45,430	106,606	135,086	130,774	145,641
Bank loan £	6,000	14,000	12,000	10,000	13,000	11,000	10,000	7,000	-		

presumably with the intention of completing the work before the
winter set in. This prompted someone, allegedly from Llanberis, to
inform local newspapers that the railway was acting on the
instruction of the Ministry of Transport. N. R. Davies wrote to
deny the claim, saying that the work was being carried out on
Sadler's recommendation and that its implementation had been
delayed by the late receipt of materials.

Hitherto unknown parts of the business came to light as
company accounts became more detailed during the 1970s.
A chalet and Welsh craft shop in Llanberis, perhaps a successor
of the Welsh woollens enterprise of 1934, made profits until
1981, when the entry disappeared following another change in
accounts presentation. Expenses for two flats at Evan Davies &
Company's office at 5 Catherine Place, London SW1, appeared
in the revenue accounts for the same period, mostly incurring
small losses tempered with an occasional small profit. Gillian
Davies used one of them for a while.

During times of strong winds services were, and still are,
terminated at Clogwyn. Even then, there are still occasions
when the wind is too strong for the trains. To maximise revenue
on such occasions a concrete platform was built in the sheltered
location known as Rocky Valley; Boyd (see Bibliography) dates
its introduction to 1974. At some as yet unidentified date a
single platform was installed at Clogwyn to assist passengers of
trains terminating there.

The 1970s were also good years for the shareholders, with
12% dividend paid in 1972 and 14% in 1973. Underlying this
apparent success, however, were serious financial problems, with
a bank overdraft of £8,107 in 1972, reaching £145,641 in 1982
(p83). Losses of nearly £40,000 were made in 1979 and 1980

84

Above: **A train climbs away from Clogwyn in 1953.**
Valentine/Author's collection

Below: **A different perspective from a little higher up.**
W. Eric Edwards/Author's collection

and no dividend was paid in 1980-2. The business was increasingly in hock to the Midland Bank: a floating charge on the undertaking from 27 August 1975; a mortgage secured on the summit property on 2 May 1980; a mortgage on the land at Llanberis on 14 May 1980; a chattels mortgage secured on the rolling stock on 31 December 1980 and a legal charge on the summit business on 21 February 1983. It is a wonder that the bank did not have the business restyled as Snowdon Mountain Railway (Midland Bank) plc. Of 1983, the directors said every effort had been made to contain overheads and improve cash flow.

N. R. Davies celebrated his 65th birthday on 27 May 1975 and was presented with an inscribed copy of a book based on the summit visitors' books signed by 51 employees. He resigned as secretary on 1 January 1978, when he was replaced by Anthony Constantine Joseph. The latter was replaced by James Ralph Woollard Hyde from 1 April 1980. Crowe died on 8 September 1983.

Jackson had retired as manager in June 1981 and then as a director on 23 March 1984; he was replaced by Derek Rogerson in both appointments, the latter also taking over as managing director in November 1984. Hyde resigned as secretary on 9 July 1984, and was replaced by A. O. E. Davies, and Whelen ceased to be a director the next day. Pursuant of the 1980 Companies Act, the company had been re-registered as a public limited company on 30 March 1982. Rogerson was to say that he found the railway in a very poor state and struggling to keep going. He introduced a five-year plan to deal with arrears of maintenance, and behind the scenes, a solution was at hand.

During the 1970s the company came under increasing criticism concerning the summit building and its surroundings. Used by 500,000 people a year, only a quarter of whom were passengers, the building was in very poor condition. Improvements had been made in 1954, 1965 and 1968, but the piecemeal approach was not the best way to deal with a building that had become tired and which was being used beyond its

No 3 rolls down the hill towards Clogwyn. *Commercial postcard/ Author's collection*

capacity. The Countryside Commission published a report in 1977, commenting not just on the building but on the 'worn out' footpaths and excessive litter. A desirable long-term aim, said the commission, was a new building.

Gillian Davies was to recall that the directors were rather hurt by the constant criticism. She related how every year, when railway personnel went to re-open the building after the winter they always found it seriously vandalised.

The company, of course, did not have the £1 million it was then estimated to require spending on the old one. Increasing pressure to improve the situation resulted in the non-railway land and building being transferred to Gwynedd County Council, and the company taking it back on a 999-year lease on 31 January 1983. The transfer of ownership allowed the council to invest in the property whilst it was managed by the railway, the length of the lease allowing the company to borrow against it. As rent, the railway was to pay 7½% of gross revenue, excluding VAT, from retail sales. The sale price was merely enough to cover the cost of conveyancing. The last of its three hotels, the company had made no capital gain from any of them.

An event of national significance impacted on the railway in 1981. A few days before the marriage of Prince Charles to Lady Diana Spencer on 29 July the SMR was subject to a vandalism attack by unknown persons believed to be protesting about the wedding. At Hebron, the points were tampered with, bolts removed from the track, a store was broken into and sleepers strewn about. The damage was seen by the permanent way gang and put right before the train service started.

Sometime in the late 1970s Nigel Keith Ross, a commercial estate agent carrying out a rent review against a client of N. R. Davies's, was intrigued by a display of SMR books and memorabilia that he saw in the latter's office. Learning that the Davies family effectively owned the railway he asked if he could buy it. This, he told the author, despite having 'no passion for steam' or interest in railways. The offer was rebuffed. The review took some time, however, and the pair continued to meet. By 1983 they were discussing the possibility of finding a new owner for the SMR. In February Ross produced Edward

Left: **No 2 at the summit in October 1951. The SIS carriage has had some glazing installed around the coupé.**
Hugh Ballantyne

Below: **By October 1951 the end wall of the summit building had been rebuilt, eliminating two of the original doors.**
Hugh Ballantyne

St George, then chairman of the Grand Bahama Port Authority, as a possible candidate but Davies was not certain that he wanted to sell. St George would have to pay a price that recognised that Davies was not an anxious seller, explained Ross, and would want to keep the Davies management team in place because he knew nothing about railways.

Nothing came of this suggestion but on 9 April 1984 Ross informed Davies that he and his partner Andrew Ian Jaye together with Brian Ivan Leaver were about to take control of Cadogan Properties Ltd, 'a substantial private property company', assets included the Tivoli shopping centre at Yardley, Birmingham, and all were interested 'in becoming involved' with the SMR.

Davies obviously knew that the company needed capital that it could not generate from revenue. The bank must have had confidence in the business to have agreed the charges and mortgages, but it was going to require a fundamental turnaround to satisfy them and to re-equip the railway. Ross knew how it could be done.

Negotiations continued during the year and Ross's formal offer was made on 10 September. Davies would remain as chairman, and own shares; Rogerson would become joint managing director; the 1954 Bentley owned by the company would be sold to Davies for £200. The offer for the share capital, at £1.15 per share, was made on 31 October 1984; it closed on 23 November 1984. The largest holdings were those of the Davies family, 163,478 shares, 58% of the issued capital, and the Crowe family, 32,000 shares, 11.43%. Company law specialist David Crowe, Crowe's son, advised the Davies family. On the second date, G. E. Davies and N. P. Evelyn stood down from the board and Ross and Jaye and Leaver were appointed to it. Jaye took over as secretary from A. O. E. Davies.

Ninety years of independence had come to an end and the SMR was now a wholly-owned subsidiary of Cadogan. The years ahead were to see a major revitalisation of the railway's fortunes.

Just before the takeover bid, on 29 October 1984, the old directors appointed N. R. Davies executive chairman for life, with a salary of £7,000, and agreed a £25,000 single-premium contribution towards his pension. These actions had had the approval of the Ross team. Just to wrap things up concerning the outgoing regime, a 6% dividend was paid for 1984; 4% had been paid for 1983.

The change of control took effect with a board meeting held on 16 November 1984. The Cadogan directors together with N. R. Davies, A. O. E. Davies and Rogerson formed an executive board. Gillian Davies continued as a non-executive director and was joined by Alexander Donald Mackay, an insurance broker, on 11 January 1985; the latter was to resign on 8 November 1987. The company's registered office was transferred back to Llanberis from 1 January 1985.

The new owners quickly introduced plans for putting the SMR on a sound financial footing. On 11 January 1985, the share capital was restructured: the 30,000 unissued 6% £1 preference shares became 120,000 25p shares; the capital was increased and reorganised to be £200,000 divided into 2,000,000 10p shares by consolidating every two existing 25p shares into one 50p share and sub-dividing those into five 10p shares – railway history does not get more complicated than this – the purpose of the restructuring was to make the shares more affordable when they were sold. Before the shares were divided, seven Davies family members, Rogerson and Elizabeth Hughes, who ran the office at Llanberis, reinvested in the business by subscribing to a total of

Right: **This 1955 view of the 20-year old summit building shows that all the window openings had been made smaller, detracting from the architect's vision for the building. The aerials on the roof are probably part of the equipment installed by the BBC in 1954. In all probability, the summit cairn had been reduced in size at the same time as the old buildings were demolished in 1938.** *Valentine/Author's collection*

Below: **A view of the station from the roof in 1953.** *Valentine/Author's collection*

25,000 of the new 25p shares at £1.15 each. New articles of association were also adopted on the same date.

On 23 January 1985, these moves were followed by the launch of a prospectus offering 840,000 10p shares for sale at 80p each. Offered under the 1983 Finance Act's business expansion scheme, this gave tax relief to investors who left their investment in place for five years; the issue was oversubscribed and closed in eight days. Cadogan held 43.3% of the issued capital; the three Davies directors together spoke for 45,000 10p shares. (The 25p shares bought for £1.15 would have been worth £2.00 each: 2 x 25p shares = 1 x 50p share = 5 x 10p shares = 5 x 80p = £4.00 ÷ 2 = £2.00.)

The purpose of the new capital was to buy two new diesel locomotives, install new sidings and improve passenger facilities. Prospective subscribers were told that on fine days in July and August demand often could not be met. Capacity was limited by

the seven steam locomotives and was reduced if one was out of service. Further, they were inflexible and could not be put into service at short notice to cope with unexpected demand. The new locomotives would cost £428,830; £42,830 from current resources, £60,000 from a Wales Tourist Board grant, £226,000 from a commercial loan and the balance from the issue. The balance of the proceeds of the issue would be used to extend, by acquisition, the company's activities in the tourist field, making it less susceptible to the vagaries of the weather.

The possibility of acquiring diesel locomotives, incidentally, had first been considered by the SMR before the takeover, Rogerson had established that the WTB might be willing to make a grant of £100,000 towards the estimated £500,000 cost of two locomotives, a carriage and a siding. The formal application for a grant had been made on 15 October 1984 and £60,000 had been awarded.

The new capital allowed the overdraft and mortgages obtained from the Midland Bank between 1975 and 1983 to be satisfied, a process that was completed by 15 January 1986. A new floating charge on the business was to be created on 9 February 1987.

During 1985 and 1986 the Cadogan directors pursued the possibility of developing a Llanberis visitor centre in partnership with the Victoria Hotel and using land owned by the SMR, the hotel and the county council. It would have contained an information centre, shops and cafés and acted as a reception centre for the attractions in Llanberis, including the pumped-storage power station, Dolbadarn Castle, the slate museum, the Llanberis Lake Railway and the SMR. Finding that neither the Central Electricity Generating Board, owners of the power station, nor the Arfon Borough Council would support the scheme it was abandoned. The architect's claim for £56,000 plus VAT as fees for the feasibility study went to court, judgment to be given in the SMR's favour in 1991.

In 1985, an attempt had been made to expand the rail business by taking over the Llanberis Lake Railway, the 2ft-gauge tourist railway running on the trackbed of the former 4ft-gauge Padarn Railway. At a very well-attended extraordinary general meeting held on 25 May, the LLR shareholders resolved to alter the company's articles to require share transfers only at the directors' discretion for a period of five years, blocking the bid. To overcome any problems with shareholders who wished to realise the value of their shares, the company also took power to buy them back, paying a substantial premium.

One diversification/expansion plan that did proceed was the acquisition of the former military airstrip, Caernarfon Airport, at Dinas Dinlle. It was purchased on a 125-year lease from the Glynllifon Estate Trust on 1 February 1986. The price was £140,000 and included equipment owned by the previous operator. The control tower was refurbished and a new operations building built. The business was operated by a subsidiary, Snowdon Mountain Aviation Ltd. A flying school was started and leisure flights using a De Havilland Rapide aircraft were offered. The SMR's articles were amended on 1 May 1987 to include the carriage of passengers by air.

For a few years from 1985, the SMR's links with Llanberis were highlighted by sponsoring Llanberis Athletic Football Club, a member of the Gwynedd League. Then one of the most consistently successful clubs in the league, it was renamed Locomotive Llanberis for the duration of the sponsorship.

The 320hp diesel locomotives were delivered from Hunslet in April 1986. Their unusual appearance, with their exposed engines and revolving jackshafts, can be explained by Rogerson's desire, he told the author later, to have locomotives with character, that were as much a visual attraction as their steam counterparts. He explained that Rolls-Royce engines were specified because most passengers would recognise the significance of the 'RR' motif on the bonnet. They proved to be ideally suited to the work required of them. The five-year loan of £225,947 obtained from Lombard North Central plc was registered on 2 May 1986.

The refurbishment of the buildings at Llanberis, including construction of an arrivals platform, was carried out in 1986 at a cost of £65,000. Refurbishment of the summit complex carried out by the county council at the same time included installing a new heating system and increasing the café's seating capacity.

At the time of the takeover the company employed 53 personnel, eight on management and administration, 37 on railway operations, and eight on ancillary services. In 1987, a funded defined-benefits pension scheme for the employees was set up with Equitable Life Assurance.

The derailment of No 7 100yd from the summit on 13 August 1987 was found to have been caused by a motion rod failing. Tests found faults in the steel used in its manufacture. The railway's regime of non-destructive testing motion components was increased and some parts were redesigned to increase their strength. A report of the accident in the *Caernarfon & Denbigh Herald* claimed that the locomotive ran away both 250yd and 250 metres. The loco crew, John McAvennie and Nigel Day, jumped off, the latter banging his

A 1961 view of the SMR's Llanberis station seen from the Victoria Hotel. *Valentine/Author's collection*

ENTRANCE TO SNOWDON MOUNTAIN RAILWAY, LLANBERIS   W 7976

Top: **No 7 waits for its carriage to be loaded in 1959.** *Valentine/ Author's collection*

Right: **Blockman Arfonwy Jones in the cabin at Hebron, September 1989.**

Below: **Train stopped in section. Something has happened because, as well as those standing near the train, there are a lot of people walking on the track behind it. The carriage is No 8.** *Frith/Author's collection*

nose, the only injury sustained. The next day trains terminated at Clogwyn while No 7 was recovered.

The air museum built at the airport in 1988/9 was funded by a rights issue that raised £158,795 from shareholders. They were offered £68 of 3% convertible unsecured loan stock for every 500 shares held. The stock was convertible into ordinary 10p shares at 80p each until 31 July 1996. Any stock not converted by 31 July 1996 would be redeemed at par on 31 July 1997. Intended as an all-weather attraction at the airport, the SMR had obtained a £44,000 grant from the WTB towards the museum's £200,000 cost. The airport had accumulated losses of £676,902 by 31 December 1991 and when the business was sold on 28 February 1992 there was a cash inflow of £43,150.

Ninian Davies, a director since 1941 and chairman since 1963, died on 3 November 1989. Rogerson sent a special bulletin to shareholders with the news. The author remembers a man of great intellect. David Crowe remembers attending

company meetings held in Davies's office and being treated to lunch afterwards. His daughter was to tell how he would stand in the one place in the garden of his house in Abersoch where Snowdon was visible and try to guess if the railway was having a good day. Ross took his place as chairman with immediate effect and formally from 23 January 1990. Elizabeth Hughes had replaced Jaye as secretary on 8 December 1989.

Writing on 6 December 1989, Rogerson told the shareholders that the railway had carried 120,826 passengers during the year, the first time more than 100,000 had been carried. The number of trains operated was also a record at 2,243, the first time that more than 2,000 had been operated. Daniel McDermid of Glasgow was presented with a free lifetime pass for travel on the railway for being the 100,000th passenger.

Several more additions to the rolling stock were made after the diesel locomotives had been delivered in 1986. In 1988, a new carriage was delivered by East Lancashire Coach Builders Ltd. Built to the limit of the SMR's loading gauge, it seats 56 passengers, has a centre gangway, which means that it has fewer doors, and wheelchair access. A five-year loan from Forward Trust Ltd was registered on 11 April 1988. A third diesel locomotive was delivered in April 1991. Built to the same design as the first two, it had been ordered from Hunslet and was built at

Top: **Trains at Clogwyn. No 8 waits in the loop for two trains descending.**
Frith/Author's collection

Left: **Summit terminus; the gradient in the station is 1 in 20. The white building next to the platform is the generator house installed in 1963.** *Author's collection*

Right: **A train arriving at the summit station, seen from the building's roof. The carriage is Lancaster No 2.**
Salmon/Author's collection

Below: **Clearing snow from the track by hand during the 1960s.**
Gillian Davies collection

Below right: **Gillian Davies, August 2009.**

Andrew Barclay's Kilmarnock works. With a contracted price of £238,512, it was financed with a £200,000 loan from Lombard North Central plc that was to be satisfied on 29 February 2000. A fourth locomotive obtained in 1992 appeared not to require any external financing.

The diesel locomotives increased the SMR's capacity, being able to make four return trips in a day as opposed to the steam locomotives' three. Their 'instant start' enabled the railway to run more trains on fine days. The maximum number of workings became 10 steam and 14 diesel trains per day. In 1993, good weather and four steam and four diesel locomotives in traffic enabled the carriage of 131,500 passengers – the best year recorded.

The advent of diesel traction was not the end for the steam fleet, though. A new boiler was obtained for No 2 in 1992 and in 1994 two more boilers were ordered. Experiments with oil firing were started in 1992, using No 4 as a testbed. Another system was tried in the same loco from 2000; the need for further development and the rising cost of oil saw the loco revert to coal burning during 2002. There had previously been an oil-firing trial involving Nos 3 and 8 in 1971/2. Experiments with draughting saw a Lempor exhaust ejector installed on No 4 in 1994, but this was removed some years later.

A more radical approach to improving the railway's capacity problems was taken in 1994, when an order was placed with HPE Tredegar Ltd for three diesel-electric railcars. With seats for 108 passengers, plus wheelchair space, the railcar train would have twice the capacity of a steam or diesel train and only need a crew of two. The increase in capacity would be significant. Working four trips per day, the railcars could increase the number of daily trains to the equivalent of 32, or 1,800 passengers.

Designed to be operated in multiple, the first railcar was delivered on 15 May 1995, the second a few days later, and the third in September. They carried their first fare-paying passengers in October. The contract price was £483,613 and Lombard North Central plc provided £360,000 of finance. Unfortunately, the builder had been placed in liquidation by the time the third vehicle had been delivered and was unable to meet its obligations for on-going warranty support after commissioning.

After an initial problem with vibration in the passenger saloons was resolved by fitting additional friction dampers, the three cars ran together on 'quite a few occasions' recalled general manager Anthony Hopkins, speaking to the author in 2009. There were, however, continuing problems with the vehicles' electronic systems, they would shut down for no obvious reason, which were never satisfactorily resolved. On two days in 1996, a record was created when the railway operated 31 out of its theoretical maximum of 32 trains, a feat that was only possible by running four trips with the three railcars. The previous record for one day, incidentally, had been 23 trains worked by five steam and two diesel locomotives in 1987.

The first of the extra sidings forecast in the prospectus was built on the opposite side of the line to the loco shed in 1985, the first new rack laid for 90 years. The need to remove rock to create level ground made it particularly expensive. The second, longer, siding was to be built in 1995 to accommodate the railcars. Simultaneously, an area of hard-standing spanning both tracks was created to aid maintenance. Other works carried out during the 1990s included repointing the arches of the viaducts and installing mile posts, the latter task completed in 1997.

The crossing equipment at Hebron was automated in 1991, with a wind turbine providing the power to operate the points and signals. Someone passing by must have guessed that the 60 amp cable used on the installation contained a lot of copper, for it and the generator were stolen during the following winter. When the Halfway loop was automated in 1995 two turbines were used to reduce the amount of cable needed. These installations used trackside switches triggered by a striker bar

Top right: **A souvenir ticket issued to mark the Queen's Silver Jubilee in 1977.** *Author's collection*

Below: **No 9, the first diesel locomotive, being delivered in April 1986.** *SMR*

mounted on the loco to detect the presence of the trains and make sure that the points were set correctly. System upgrades in 2006 saw solar panels installed to supplement the wind turbines, signals illuminated by LEDs and the points operated by remote controls worked by train guards, going uphill, and drivers, going downhill. The remote controls use coded signals on the license-free 433MHz radio frequency. The four-wire system includes fault monitoring.

Rogerson retired as general manager on 1 September 1995, but remaining as managing director. His replacement was Anthony Peter Hopkins, who joined on 11 September; he had previously been a projects manager at GEC Alstom, Preston. A year later Hopkins also became managing director and Rogerson retired, maintaining his connection as a non-executive director.

Both men played a part in arranging events to mark the company's centenary in 1996. The anniversary day, 6 April, Easter Saturday, was marked by the issue of an anniversary label for the railway's summit mail (p94). A formal event took place on 21 June. Unfortunately, the intended principal guest, Lord Tonypandy, former speaker of the House of Commons, George Thomas, was ill so his place was taken by Gwilym Jones MP, secretary of state for Wales with special responsibility for transport. Rogerson calculated that the railway had carried 5½ million passengers during the previous 100 years. Guests included former railway employees and Frau Heidi Abt, wife of Peter Abt, a great-nephew of Roman Abt, the inventor of the SMR's rack system. Peter, a college lecturer, had been unable to gain leave of absence to be present.

An enthusiast event was held on 28/29 September 1996, when an all-steam service was operated and five locomotives were steamed, believed to be for the first time since 1992. The occasion saw the return to steam of No 3 *Wyddfa* after a 'part-time' overhaul that had taken two years. With a new boiler, cylinders, side rods, injectors, cab, bunker, regulator, chimney and blastpipe all being replaced this was the most intensive overhaul ever undertaken by the railway.

It was during the 1990s that Nigel Day, one of the drivers, started to decorate his loco, initially No 7 and then No 4, with various insignia, including some very ornate brass lamps. Feeling overlooked by the attention that Day's loco received, from 1996 the other drivers sought approval to decorate their locos, too. Not having his metalworking skills, they settled for painting the locos in different colours, resulting in a multi-coloured fleet, although only two of the diesel locos were repainted. The standard green livery was restored from 2001/2 although there are, at the time of writing, variations in lining.

The second of two changes in Cadogan's ownership had what might be described as unexpected consequences for the SMR. The 1993 report recorded that Cadogan was owned by

During the 1980s some consideration was given to replacing the summit building with a facility constructed in the embankment at Clogwyn. This artist's impression is dated 1989. *SMR*

Lever & Haigside Ltd, another property company in which Ross and Jaye had an interest. Then, in 1995, Cadogan was owned by Compco Holdings plc, in which Lever, Ross and Jaye had an interest. Cadogan had actually made a reverse takeover of Compco, a much larger company. As a stock exchange-listed company, Compco became aware that the market likes focused companies and could not understand why a property company should own a railway. Compco therefore came under pressure to dispose of the SMR.

A buyer was found early in 1998. Kevin Ronald Leech, then a businessman with interests in biotechnology, had diversified into landmark destinations, including Land's End and John o'Groats. At the time he was ranked 157th in the *Sunday Times* Rich List. His private company, Crockley Green Ltd, registered in Jersey, bought Compco's SMR shareholding for 74p per share and made an offer for the remainder. On 14 August 1998, Leech and three of his nominees were appointed directors, the three

Cadogan directors retiring at the same time. Leech became chairman. By the end of the year, Crockley Green owned 90% of the SMR capital, while the remainder was acquired shortly afterwards. The takeover valued the railway at £1.33 million; previously the shares had been changing hands for 50p.

The railway had been transformed during the Cadogan era, marked by new rolling stock, increased capacity, innovation and, for the employees, a pension scheme. With passengers carried ranging from 76,539 in 1986 to 156,944 in 1996, the centenary year, this surely counts as a success. Despite the failure of attempts to expand into other leisure markets, the SMR emerged well placed to face the challenges of the future.

The last years of Cadogan's involvement had been particularly good for the shareholders, too. Dividends of 2½p per share paid from 1991 until 1994 and 3p per share until 1997 equate to a remarkable 22½% and 30%! Although at 74p the shares had made a loss on the 1985 80p issue price, the realisation for those who had bought 25p shares at £1.10 was £1.85. Of his involvement with the SMR, Ross told the author in 2009 that it was a 'pride of ownership' business; he enjoyed his time with it but it was very time-consuming. The Cadogan team had visited Llanberis every six weeks during their tenure.

On 25 May 1999, the SMR was transferred to Heritage Great Britain plc, a Liverpool-based business wholly owned by Leech, via Cherberry Ltd, another Jersey-registered company, which managed all of his attractions. Snowdon Mountain Railway plc was re-registered as a private company, Snowdon Mountain Railway Ltd, on 29 June 1999. When Heritage GB was reorganised on 31 January 2000 the SMR's 'trade, assets and liabilities' were transferred to another group company, Heritage Attractions Ltd. There was now no need for the SMR company to exist and it has been registered as dormant since 1 February 2000. Ownership of Cherberry was transferred to the trustees of a Jersey-registered settlement during 2001.

Before that point had been reached, changes to the SMR board saw Rogerson resign on 9 August 1999, followed by Andrew and Gillian Davies on 30 November 1999, bringing to an end nearly 80 years of Davies family involvement with the SMR. Andrew Davies had been told that he could keep his seat on the board under the new regime but lost it when Leech gained control of more than 90% of the capital and exercised his right, under Stock Exchange rules, to acquire the remaining shares compulsorily.

The final break with the old management came in February 2001, when Hopkins was made redundant. Alan Kendall, an existing Heritage Great Britain employee who had transferred to the SMR to the review its health and safety regime in 1999, took over as general manager on 1 March and remains in post at the time of writing.

The new owners turned their attention to presentation and marketing. When the Llanberis shop was refurbished in 2000, original features of the building were revealed for the first time in many years. A small museum display was created near the arrivals platform at the same time. A new ticketing system was introduced in 2001.

Innovations on the track include construction of track panels at Llanberis to maintain quality and speed up installation and a programme of eliminating short sections of rack. Numerical markers indicate the position of every 50th rack length to aid fault reporting. By 2009 the railway had a policy of replacing 800 sleepers each year.

Conditions at the summit, meanwhile, had deteriorated beyond the capability of any remedial works to resolve them. The Prince of Wales notoriously called it 'the highest slum in Wales' or 'in Britain' or 'in England and Wales', depending on the source, as it has not been possible to identify when he said it. The earliest reference to this much-quoted remark 'the highest

slum in Europe', found by the author was published in the *Guardian* in 1974, when it was unattributed. A 1982 report, also in the *Guardian*, attributes it to 'generations of conservationists' so perhaps the Prince was quoting someone else.

However, after many years of debate a resolution of the summit building problem was started in December 2004. Planning permission for the replacement building was given for a new structure estimated to cost £8.1 million. Designed by Ray Hole, it was funded by the Snowdonia National Park Authority, the Welsh Assembly Government, the Welsh European Funding Office, Visit Wales, the SMR (£217,000), and contributors to a public appeal. The building was designed to resist the extreme weather conditions at the summit and to comply with modern environmental requirements.

Carillion plc was appointed the contractor and work started with the demolition of the old building in the autumn of 2006. The expectation was that the building would be completed during the summer of 2007 and opened in May 2008, but the loss of many days because of high winds and unseasonal snow delayed completion until September 2008. Not for the first time were confident predictions about undertaking work on the mountain overturned by the weather.

As might be expected, the project had a considerable effect on the railway. All passenger trains were terminated at Clogwyn during 2007 and 2008, and its car park became a works site compound. At Llanberis, a bridge was built over the Afon Hwch to give vehicular access to the railway from the car park for loading. Also bridging the river, the railcar siding was extended to the same area and connected to the main line by a remote-controlled solar-powered point, enabling loading to take place without interrupting the passenger service. With the departure of the contractors in 2009, these alterations were left in place with planning permission being granted to use the road bridge for fuel deliveries and the disposal of effluent from the summit; by October the railway was having the abutments clad in stone.

To carry all equipment and materials to the summit and all debris and waste to Llanberis, Hunslet built a 10-ton capacity 40ft flat wagon before work started in 2006. It was fitted with an electronic braking system that could be monitored and controlled from the cabs of any of the SMR's diesel locomotives. SMR engineers equipped it with a closed-circuit TV camera mounted at the front so the crew could use a cab-mounted monitor to check that the track was clear during times of poor visibility. Up to four trains a day were run for construction purposes.

Top: **The cover of a programme issued by Locomotive Llanberis during the time the local football team was sponsored by the SMR.** *Author's collection*

Left: **The SMR's centenary was celebrated on 21 June 1996. Chairman Nigel Ross, left, and Managing Director Derek Rogerson look on as Gwilym Jones MP, Secretary of State for Wales with special responsibility for transport, unveils the commemorative plaque.**

A few minutes later the Secretary of State named No 12 *George* in honour of Lord Tonypandy, the former speaker of the House of Commons, George Thomas, who had not been well enough to attend. Gwilym Jones and Derek Rogerson pose for photographs.

The railway took the view that it would benefit from the new building in the long term and did not seek compensation for the interruption to its business. In an attempt to mitigate its losses, although, a planning application was made for a temporary catering facility at Clogwyn in May 2007. This was refused as being contrary to the national park's policies. The SMR's owner, Heritage Attractions Ltd, was to attribute a revenue reduction of £80,000 during the year as mainly due to the non-availability of the outlet.

Following a period of fitting out and commissioning the building's systems, it was formally opened by the Welsh Assembly Government's first minister, Rhodri Morgan, on 12 June 2009. The railway ran four trains for the benefit of the SNPA's guests.

The new building, called Hafod Eryri, summer residence in Snowdonia, by the authority, occupies the same floor space as its predecessor, but the lack of a first floor means that it is smaller. Features include a large viewing window and a smaller window on the east wall designed to give a view of the summit. Operationally, the railway has the same two platforms as before. The building is connected to the railway's network by a wireless link between the summit and Waterfall, allowing remote control and supervision of its control and point of sale systems.

It generates much more non-operational rail traffic than before, at busy times requiring up to 10,000l of water per day and 3,000l of fuel oil every three days, making much use of the Hunslet truck

for this purpose. It is not unusual, however, to see 1,000l of water despatched in the four-wheeled wagon with a passenger train. At the summit, underground tanks accommodate 10,000l of potable water and slightly more of grey water. Storage for sewage is expected to last up to two months.

Passenger traffic during the months following the opening was extremely good with trains fully booked several days in advance. On many days 1,000 passengers were carried, against estimates of 800 a day. Would-be passengers often had to wait hours to be connected to the SMR's telephone-booking call centre and then maybe several days before they could travel. Before long the high demand caused complaints about overcrowding and other issues. There were unexpected consequences too. Space was often lost by walkers piling their bags in the centre of the café and the racks intended for bags, located in the public convenience lobby, were used to secure dogs whilst their owners used the conveniences, much to the consternation of intending users unused to dogs.

This seems to be a good point to bring this story to an end. After a difficult start, the Snowdon Mountain Railway has survived 114 years at the time of publication. It has owners and staff who care for it. The SMR will undoubtedly face many challenges in the future, but none will be greater than those it has experienced in the past.

To mark his takeover of the SMR, Kevin Leach visited Llanberis on 25 May 2000.

Above: **In connection with the summit building renewal project the railcar siding was extended over the Afon Hwch to accommodate the extra trains required by the contractors. No 4 was seen passing the new bridge on 1 August 2007.**

Left: **A view of the extended siding's connection to the main line seen from the ramp that linked the site to the car park. No 12 was returning to Llanberis on 1 August 2007. The LED signals and solar panels can be seen.**

Bottom: **On 12 October 2007 a train was laid on for members of the Snowdonia National Park Authority to see the summit works in progress. At Clogwyn it passed one of the contractors' workings returning to Llanberis.**

Top left: **The summit platform with the new plant room under construction, 12 October 2007. The building contains an office dedicated to railway operating purposes.**

Top right: **A view of the new building, called Hafod Eryri, under construction as seen from the summit and surrounded by cloud on 12 October 2007. On a clear day the line of windows on the back of the building makes the summit visible from inside.**

Right: **After the track had been relaid, No 2 worked the first train to Hafod Eryri on 2 April 2009.** *Doug Blair*

Below: **No 2 bedecked with flags after hauling one of the re-opening trains is seen at the new station on 12 June 2009.**

Above: **Hafod Eryri on 12 June 2009. A train is just visible to its left.**

Below: **No 6 and carriage No 5 propel the wagon containing 2,000 litres of water near Halfway on 13 June 2009.** *Andrew Hurrell*

Appendix 1

The mechanical equipment of the Snowdon Mountain Railway 1899

Gowrie Colquhon Aitchison, Assoc M INST CE

T he Snowdon Mountain Railway starts from Llanberis at a point some 350 feet above sea level, and ascends with varying gradients, ranging between 1 in 20 and 1 in 5.5, until it reaches the upper terminus, which lies about 50 feet below the actual summit of the mountain, which is 3,560 above sea level. The total rise of the railway from terminus to terminus is 3,140 feet, and the length is 4 miles 54 chains, the average gradient being 1 in 7.83. The system adopted is that known as the 'Abt', and the rack is used for the whole length of the line, and on all sidings and turnouts, as well as in the engine and carriage sheds. The line is single, but three passing places or turnouts are provided at practically equal distances, as well as a double track at each terminal station of sufficient length to hold a full train. The sharpest curve is of 4 chains radius.

THE SNOWDON MOUNTAIN RAILWAY: PERMANENT WAY.
SIR DOUGLAS FOX AND MR. FRANCIS FOX, WESTMINSTER, ENGINEERS.

Diagrams of SMR track produced by Fox. *Author's collection*

Permanent Way

This is of steel throughout. The bearing rails are rolled to the Indian State Railways' section; they are flanged, and weigh 41¼lb per yard. The sleepers are of rolled steel, 6ft long by 1in thick on the crown, gradually tapering off in thickness at the sides; their ends are doubled down, and they weigh 67lb each. The bearing rails are fastened to these sleepers by clips, which are fixed to the sleeper by hook bolts; each clip has a projection on its under side, which, together with the hook bolt, fits into an oblong hole through the crown of the sleeper.

The gauge is widened as required on the curves by this projection on the underside of the clip being varied in size. Sleepers are spaced regularly 2ft 11½in apart. The rack, which is double, is of mild rolled steel, and is carried down the centre of the line on rolled steel chairs weighing 12lb each, machined on the faces against which the rack bars fit. These chairs are connected to the sleeper by two finch steel bolts, the square heads of which are rigidly held on the underside of the sleeper by a channelled iron plate. Rack bars of varying strength are used, according to the steepness of the gradient: on gradients below 1 in 9, the thickness of rack bar is 20mm; on gradients of 1 in 9 and over, the thickness of rack bar is 25mm. The rack bars are 5 feet 10 inches long, and are so laid that the tooth of the bar on one side of the chair comes opposite the space of the bar on the other side. The weight per rack bar of 25mm in thickness is 67lb, and per rack bar of 20mm in thickness 53lb. All rack bars are 4⁵⁄₁₆ in in depth. Two ¾in fish bolts fasten the rack bars to each chair.

The following are the dimensions of the teeth:

Depth of tooth	50mm
Centre to centre of teeth	120mm
Length at pitch line	60mm

There is now on all gradients (but dropped off at the crossings) what may be termed a 'safety angle iron', an arrangement designed with a view to supplying an additional safeguard against the possibility of the cogs on the engine pinions mounting and thus losing or reducing their engagement with the teeth of the rack. This angle iron is of rolled steel, and attached to each side of the rack bars by the same bolts which hold the rack bars to the chairs. It is laid in various lengths to suit both vertical and horizontal curves, and dowel pins are inserted at the ends to secure correct alignment at the joints. In consequence of the variation in the thickness of the rack bars (as before described), a 5mm washer has to be introduced between the 20mm rack bar and the angle iron, in order that the latter should always be the same distance from the centre throughout. Two grippers are attached to each engine, and one, or in some cases two, to each carriage. These are so adjusted that they never come in contact with the angle iron unless there be a tendency to mount, when the gripper will at once come into action by catching under the flanges of the angle iron.

All rails, rack bars, and angle irons are fishplated. The bolt holes at the lower end of the bearing rails are round, but those at the upper end are oval, so that expansion takes place up hill. Each rack bar has four bolt holes, the two in the centre being round, while those at each end are oval, expansion being thus allowed for from the centre. To prevent creeping, iron stays or uprights are set at intervals in solid concrete blocks, and the lower side of a joint sleeper is allowed to rest against them. The spacing of these anchors depends on the steepness of the gradient. On the 1 in 6 gradients they are about 60yd apart.

The crossings adopted on the Snowdon Railway are of rather a complicated character, as the rack is carried right through, thus making a continuous track for the engine pinions. The switches are 12ft in length, the radius of curve being

151ft 3in, the rate of crossing about 1 in 4, and the angle 130. The rods and levers which work the points are connected with and work hinged portions of the rack, which are thus brought into correct position at the same time as the points are thrown over. This provides a continuous rack for the passing of the engine, and also clears a passage for the bearing wheels. No crossing is placed on a steeper gradient than 1 in 10.

Locomotives

These were built by the Schweizerische Locomotiv und Maschinenfabrik of Winterthur, Switzerland. They weigh 13 tons 5cwt when empty, and 17 tons 5cwt when in running order with full load of coal and water. They were guaranteed to be capable of driving a load of 18 tons up a gradient of 1 in 5 at a speed of 67km per hour. Their IHP is 166. The cylinders are 300mm in diameter, and they are placed outside the frame. The stroke is 600mm. The motion is communicated to the cranks by means of a one sided rocking lever with upper and lower connecting rods. The throw of the cranks is thus reduced and tractive power increased. The fulcrum of the rocking lever is kept as low as possible. The valve chests are above the cylinders. There are three axles, the leading and second each having pinion wheels attached, and being coupled together, while the third is on a trailing pony truck.

The wheels are carried inside the frames, and are all loose on the axles except one of those on the trailing axle, which is keyed. The first and second axles have solid forged disks in their centres; to each of these disks are attached two steel pinion rings, so set that their teeth alternate. There are 15 teeth to each pinion ring. In order to hold these pinion rings in their relative position on the axle disks, and yet at the same time to allow some slight circumferential movement to prevent jarring, and also to allow for any slight irregularity in the pitch of the teeth of the rack bars, eight double horseshoe springs are inserted in the disk under each pinion ring. The upper ends of these springs project into countersunk spaces on the inner or under side of the rings. The maximum play allowed is 3mm, and to avoid more play being obtained in the event of one of these springs snapping or becoming weak, a solid iron tongue is introduced. The springs and pinion rings are held in position by the brake drums (which will afterwards be described), being placed on each side, and being firmly bolted through the solid forged axle disks with eight steel bolts 1in in diameter.

THE TRACK, SNOWDON MOUNTAIN RAILWAY SMR 4

The teeth of the pinions on the leading axle are given a lead over those on the second axle of one quarter the distance between two teeth, in order that when the teeth of a pinion on the leading axle are about to leave engagement with the rack, the teeth of the corresponding pinion on the second axle are about to engage. Perfect and continuous engagement is thus secured. In order to

101

keep the water level over the crown of the firebox as regular as possible, the whole boiler is set down by the head at a slope of 1 in 11 to the horizontal. The gauge glasses are placed halfway along the boiler, so as to register correctly on the varying gradients.

Gauge of rails	800mm	2ft 7 in
Diameter of cylinders	300mm	11 1¹⁄₁₆in
Stroke of piston	600mm	1ft 11⅝in
Diameter of pinion wheels at pitch circle	573mm	22.56in
Pitch of teeth		4.72in
Diameter of rail wheels on coupled axles	653mm	25.71in
Diameter of truck wheels	520mm	20.74in
Wheel base, rigid	1,350mm	4ft 5ft⅛in
Wheel base, total, total	3,000mm	9ft 10⅛in

Boiler

Number of tubes	156	
Inside diameter of tubes	32mm	1.26in
Outside diameter of tubes	35mm	1.38in
Heating surface, fire box	3.90sq m	41.981sq ft
Heating surface, tubes	33.00sq m	355.220sq ft
Heating surface, total	36.90sq m	397.200sq ft
Grate area	0.95	10.030sq ft
Steam pressure when at work	14kg per sq cm	200lb per sq in
Hydraulic test pressure	20kg per sq cm	284.4lb per sq in
Plates, cylindrical shell	11mm	0.43in
Plates, copper fire box	14mm	055in
Plates, tube plates	25mm	0.98 and
	20mm	0.79in
Feed water in tanks	1,700l	374gal
Cooling water for brake	300l	66gal
Coal box capacity	500kg	10cwt
Water in boiler	1,150l	253gal
Coal in fire box, and tools	400kg	88lb
Maximum load per axle	6,000kg	5.90 tons
Tractive power	7,100kg	7 tons

The boiler plates are of mild steel, the firebox is of copper with a circular top, and the tubes are of steel with copper ends at the firebox end. The water tanks are on either side of the boiler, and run the whole length of the same. The leading dimensions of the engines are given in the table.

A most careful test was applied to samples of all the materials used in the construction of these engines. The cost of the engines averaged about £1,475 each.

The two grippers are placed one in front of the leading axle and the other between the first and second axles in the centre of the engine.

Brakes — there are five brakes on each engine: two separate hand brakes, one steam brake which can be applied by hand, one automatic brake, and one air brake.

Handbrake — on each of the driving axles (on each side of the pinions and securely bolted direct on to the axle disks previously referred to) are two deeply grooved cast steel brake drums, upon which grooved cast iron brake blocks work, one on each side of each drum, thus there are four drums with eight brake blocks, the working face area of each block being 60sq in. These blocks are actuated by hand from the cab, there being two handles, one for the driver, which operates the four blocks on the right-hand side of the engine, and one for the fireman, which operates the four blocks on the left-hand side.

Steam brake — in addition to the handbrake arrangement described above, the four blocks on the right-hand side of the engine are capable of being worked by steam, the driver being able to bring them into action by means of a hand lever rod, conveniently placed over the crown of the firebox.

Automatic brake — this is a brake which is designed to come into action automatically in the event of an engine travelling, from any cause, above a given speed. On the right-hand side of the frame plate is placed a circular cast iron box, which is connected to a small shaft which passes through to the inside of the frame plate and is there geared by means of toothed wheels direct to the leading axle. Within the circular box is a governor block, to which a light coil spring is attached; this spring is controlled by a screw which may be tightened or loosened, and thus regulates the action of the governor block. On the maximum or limit of speed allowed being exceeded, the nose of this governor block projects sufficiently far to strike a trigger, which, on being tripped releases a powerful coil spring, and this, in its turn, pulls down a rod which opens a cone valve, and steam is admitted gradually into the steam brake cylinder, which is fixed on the inside of the engine frame. This arrangement has to be most carefully adjusted and constantly tested as it is absolutely essential that the action of this brake should not be sudden, as locking of the pinions too quickly must be carefully avoided on such gradients as those on the Snowdon Railway. Before the engine can proceed, after this brake has come into action, it is necessary for the driver to leave the cab and put the lever back in position and reset the trigger and so cut off the ingress of steam.

Air brake — this brake is used to control the engine while descending the mountain. Air is admitted to the cylinders through the exhaust ports, and on becoming compressed controls the travel of the piston. The driver, in order to allow the engine to descend, allows the compressed air to escape through a hand valve, which is conveniently placed at the rear of the cab. All steam is cut off when the engine is descending, and when the air inlet to the exhaust ports is open the passage for the steam exhaust to the chimney is closed. To avoid excessive wear and tear, water is taken into the cylinder along with the air, from a spray pipe. This brake is most effective in its action, completely controlling the engine without the aid of other brake power, as long as everything in connection with it is kept in absolute repair, and all leakage is reduced to a minimum.

The author [Aitchison] at first found it extremely difficult to accurately control the speed at which the drivers allowed their engines to travel; he therefore had 'speed indicators' attached to each engine. These instruments indicate the speed by a hand on a plain dial face, and in addition ring one beat on a gong to warn the driver that he is approaching his limit of speed, and three

beats when he has reached or exceeded that limit. These indicators also register, by means of pin pricks on a paper roll, the variations of speed during the journey, and so an accurate record can be kept of each driver's performances. The instrument has the appearance of a clock and is fixed on the top of the right-hand side watertank, and directly facing the driver. A down shaft runs from the indicator, through the tank, to a box or case which is supported by bolts to the engine frame; within this box are a pair of mitre wheels, one keyed to the down shaft, the other to a short shaft which projects through the side of the box, and at the end of which is a crank with a long slot. This crank is worked by a projecting pin connected to the crank of the

second driving axle, the revolutions of the axle being thus transmitted to the indicator. The engines are fitted with right and left-hand re-starting injectors and sight lubricators for the cylinders and valve chests; there is also an oil dripper arrangement in the cab which conveys a heavy lubricating oil direct to the teeth of the pinion wheels, but this is not sufficient in itself, and it is therefore essential that the rack bars are kept thoroughly lubricated. If this is carefully attended to there is little wear and tear on either the pinion wheel or the rack, considering the work these engines have to accomplish during a season.

The coal consumption is heavy, the quantity used varying considerably with the load taken up and the quality of the coal.

Above: **A view of the loco shed and yard seen from the lifting gantry on 29 March 1997. A small machine shop is located behind the water tank. All the railcars are in the picture, two of them entering the station.**

Left: **This busy scene from May 1980 demonstrates the less-than-optimum conditions for the SMR's workshop staff. The first lifting gantry is being used to replace No 6's cab and the work has to take place on the main line in between passing trains.**

Unfortunately this last year, owing to trade complications, no really reliable tests could be carried out; but it is a fair average to say that from 6cwt to 7cwt of good quality quick steaming coal is burned on one journey.

The carriages are 38ft long over buffers, 6ft 6in wide and 9ft 4in high; they are open at the sides above the door level, and are divided into seven compartments, each holding eight persons, and a separate compartment in front for the guard.

Canvas curtains are provided for use in wet weather, hung on slender wooden rods, which would snap under very severe strain from wind. In order to obviate any discomfort to the passengers, owing to the gradients up which the carriages have to pass, the upper seats in each compartment are deeply hollowed on the sitting portion; by this simple arrangement the necessity of stepping the floor of the carriage, or having movable seats, has been avoided. The weight of each carriage is 5 tons 13cwt now that grippers have been fitted similar to those on the engines. The underframe is of light sections of channel steel. The two four-wheeled bogies are spaced 28ft centre to centre, the wheelbase of each bogie being 4ft; the wheels are of cast steel on steel axles.

On the rear bogie in each carriage is a double brake pinion, which is carried on a separate short axle in the centre of the bogie frame, between the two bearing axles, and to the outer sides of which are bolted two grooved brake drums, on which

Left: **A pair of loco wheelsets. The pinions last 18 months in service. 1 September 1992.**

Below: **On 6 June 1999, one of the locos had its boiler stripped of fittings ready for renewal.**

four cast iron brake blocks operate. These blocks are applied by hand by the guard, from his compartment at the front end of the carriage, by means of a wheel. This brake arrangement is similar to the hand brakes on the locomotives. The claw, or gripper, is carried at the back of the rear bogie. The centre of gravity of the carriages has been kept as low as possible, in consequence of the strong and gusty winds experienced on the mountain. A carriage with its full complement of passengers is calculated to withstand a wind pressure of 36lb per sq ft. No couplings are ever used except to draw carriages out of the sheds.

The goods wagons are 12ft long and 6ft 3in wide, the sides being 11in deep. The under frames are of channel steel and the wheels and axles of steel; the distance from centre to centre of wheels is 7ft, and each wagon is constructed to carry 6 tons. A platform is provided for the conductor, with a hand or guard rail, to which the brake wheel is fixed. The wagon brake is similar in action to those on the carriages, but the pinion wheels and brake drums are attached direct to the rear axle.

The brakes, both on the carriages and wagons, are exceedingly powerful in action, completely controlling the carriage when applied on the steepest gradient. They are never applied except in case of emergency.

Top: **A braked carriage bogie under maintenance in June 1992.**

Below: **Railcar No 22 had its power bogie removed for attention, on 21 June 1996.**

Bottom: **A view inside the loco shed with the nearly completed carriage ambulance bogie in the foreground.**

Top: Three generations on SMR motive power lined up on 21 June 1996, the day the railway celebrated its centenary.

Left: The varied colours of the locomotives were a feature of the later 1990s, Nos 3, 6 and 2 being photographed on 16 April 2001; the return to a standard livery was started shortly afterwards.

Bottom left: In August 1989 the train works was seen at Llanberis being loaded loading with ballast.

Bottom right: No 8 being taken up the line on test on 23 August 1984. The spikes with warning triangles were carried on the locos to be dropped off if the loco crew noticed a track defect.

Appendix 2
Locomotives and rolling stock

Locomotives and railcars

There is no record of the original locomotive livery and none of the early writers thought to make any mention of it. Where the locomotive is visible in some of the early, late 19th century, coloured postcards they look black. In 1933, Davies reported that a red line had been added (p69). Kidner (see Bibliography for references to this section) contains the earliest reference to livery found by the author, in 1937 saying that the locomotives

Number	Name	Wheel arrangement	Date built	Builder's No	Remarks
1	L. A. D. A. S.	0-4-2T Rack	1895	923	Boiler No 1,544. Named for Laura Alice Duff Assheton-Smith. Destroyed on 6 April 1896.
2	Enid	0-4-2T Rack	1895	924	Boiler No 1,545. Named for Enid Assheton-Smith who cut the first sod on 15 December 1894. SMR personnel pronounce the name Ennid. Rebuilt by Hunslet in 1958, works number 58833 allocated. Dark blue livery from 1998.
3	Wyddfa	0-4-2T Rack	1895	925	Rebuilt by Hunslet in 1960, works number 58948 allocated. In 1988 the author was told that No 3 had been renamed Yr Wyddfa but photographic evidence reveals that this was not the case. In-house overhaul completed in 1996, when it was painted maroon.
4	Snowdon	0-4-2T Rack	1896	988	Rebuilt by Hunslet in 1963, works number 59092 allocated. Rebuilt by Hunslet again in 1978. Brunswick green livery in 1990s.
5	Moel Siabod	0-4-2T Rack	1896	989	Rebuilt by Hunslet in 1959, works number 58889 allocated. Chocolate brown livery applied in 1997 faded, repainted black in 2000. Out of use since 2001.
6	Padarn	0-4-2T Rack	1922	2838	Named Sir Harmood until 1923. Black livery in 1997.
7	Ralph	0-4-2T Rack	1923	2869	Named Aylwin until 4 October 1978 when renamed Ralph Sadler after the SMR's late consulting civil engineer. Renamed Ralph 2 May 1987. Out of use since c1990.
8	Eryri	0-4-2T Rack	1923	2870	Out of use since c1992.
9	Ninian	0-4-0DH Rack	1986	9249	Named by N. R. Davies, then chairman of the company, in recognition of the Davies family's involvement with the SMR since 1922, on 2 May 1987.
10	Yeti	0-4-0DH Rack	1986	9250	Named by Rhonda Golding of Bristol on 2 May 1987. The name was chosen following a competition run on BBC TV's Breakfast Time programme, winning a life pass for travel on the railway for Ms Golding. The locomotive is 'dedicated to all creatures on the mountain living and legendary'. Painted purple in the 1990s.
11	Peris	0-4-0DH Rack	1991	9305/775	Ordered from Hunslet and built by Barclay; both companies allocated works numbers. Named after a local saint on 22 August 1992.
12	George	0-4-0DH Rack	1992	9312	Named after George Thomas, Viscount Tonypandy, former speaker of the House of Commons, by Gwilym Jones MP on 21 June 1996. Mauve livery in the 1990s.
21		Railcar	1995	1074	Out of use at time of publication.
22		Railcar	1995	1075	Out of use at time of publication.
23		Railcar	1995	1076	Out of use at time of publication.

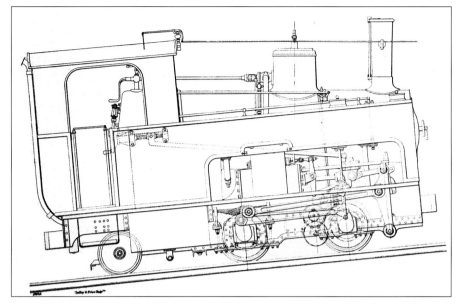

Left: **Elevation of the first SMR locomotives, as built.** *Author's collection*

Below: **A similar diagram showing the internal layout.** *Author's collection*

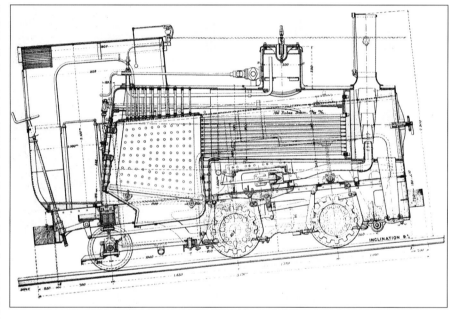

were painted black; as he had visited the railway in 1935 this report has the benefit of being based on personal observation. Photographs are of no assistance because orthochromatic film would not distinguish the two colours.

However, when enthusiast L. W. Perkins visited the railway in 1942 he photographed No 2 inside the shed, noting that it was out of service and painted and lined in green. As painting to this standard was unlikely to be carried out during wartime it must be assumed that it dated to the late 1930s. During the 1950s some locomotives had silver smokebox doors and a colour transparency of unknown date exists showing No 8 with its cab painted brown edged in black, its boiler barrel smokebox and frames painted black, bufferbeam red and chimney and smokebox door painted silver. The earliest dated colour photographs showing SMR locomotives in what became the standard green livery, were taken in 1961; Jones (see Bibliography) saw Nos 5 and 8 like this in May.

The locomotives' small fireboxes were designed to burn dry steam coal. Traditionally, the Ministry of Fuel & Power defined dry steam coal as being non-caking, with 10 to 13.5% volatile matter and an ash fusion temperature of more than 1,300°C. Coal of this specification is no longer mined in the UK and the definition was widened to include coals with 14 to 14.5% volatiles with some caking properties and ash fusion above 1,200°C, a point at which the ash fusion temperature becomes critical on the SMR locomotives. The following information illustrated the situation in 1988: Onllwyn Colliery in South Wales provided the best coal for SMR purposes but switched to anthracite. Deep Navigation coal was now the first choice, followed by Daw Mill (although Daw Mill was not a dry steam coal, having volatiles above 30%, it was non-caking and had an acceptable ash fusion temperature). A combination of the two coals was normally burnt in the sequence, from Llanberis, first Deep Navigation, then Daw Mill, and then Deep Navigation, the Deep Navigation thereby being used on the steepest sections and in the area of Llanberis village itself, to reduce pollution. Primary and secondary air modifications were tried before without success. British Coal fuel technologists

investigated the SMR's problems, concluding that they could only be overcome by re-designing the boilers. As an example of how critical it is for the railway to have the right fuel, the tale is told of the open-cast coal supplied during the miners' strike; the fire on No 2 went out for no obvious reason and the locomotive had to be towed back to Llanberis where investigation found that the firebox tubeplate was filled with lava from melted ash.

The SLM delivery notes for Nos 7 and 8 show that each locomotive was supplied with a comprehensive set of tools and equipment. In a packing case were: 5 paper rolls for speed recorders; 3 signal lamps with red and green discs; 2 chisels; 1 screw driver; 2 punches; 3 files; 1 syringe; 8 water gauge glasses with 16 rubber rings; 3 box keys for lubricator; 6 spanners; 3 water gauge lamps.

A 10-ton winch was packed in the cab. In the coal bunker was packed: speed recorder; whistle; hammer; copper hammer; lead hammer; monkey wrench; 4 tube plugs for smoke tubes; 4 tube plugs for boiler tubes; 2 single spanners; 4 double spanners; spanner for axlebox wedge; 2 washout plug spanners; 1 brush; 1 slack shovel; 1 slack pricker; 1 grate scraper; 1 coal shovel; 1 tube cleaner; 1 box key for drain cock; 1 water bucket.

enclosed working conditions being appreciated.

The railcars' clerestory roofs were intended to be reminiscent of traditional tramcars. They have triple-reduction gearboxes with single helical gear first and second stages and straight spurs on the final drive. The 1½ ton gear assembly mounted on the downhill bogie incorporates the rack pinion drive and brake drum and the operating gear and electric drive motor. The electronic control equipment was supplied by Alstom. The motor is supplied by an alternator driven at constant speed by a Cummins diesel engine. The engine, alternator and control system are housed within the vehicle. The uphill bogie has a brake pinion. Testing suggested that this would be inadequate on its own, leading to a prohibition on them operating singly. Within a year or two, it became a regular occurrence for one of them to be out of service due to issues with their bogies, gearboxes or electronics. Several attempts were made to find a solution but the first was taken out of service in 2001 and the others in 2003. They have been stored off-rail in the car park since 2006. Consideration is being given to returning them to service and approval has been given to replacing the inverter in one vehicle with this in mind.

Carriages and wagons

The Lancaster Carriage & Wagon Company supplied six carriages and four drop-side, two-plank wagons to the SMR in 1896. One of the carriages was returned to the maker in 1897 for conversion to an open vehicle. It was returned to Llanberis in 1898 having been made shorter and with its roof removed. Another open carriage was obtained in 1900, possibly from the Ashbury Carriage & Wagon Company. Photographs showing the opens in service are uncommon; it was probably customary to have one of them propelled in front of an ordinary train although one photograph shows a train that comprised both of them. They were taken out of service at an unknown date.

Boyd suggested that the 1911 minute approving a carriage being sent to Ince for repair actually concealed an order for a

In a toolbox were five oil cans of different sizes and shapes.

When the diesel locomotives were designed every consideration was given to interchangeability of common parts to aid integration with the steam fleet. Of the major mechanical components it proved possible to use the same pinion ring and fixing but not the wheelsets. Routine oiling round was replaced by the installation of pneumatic pump lubricators on timers. A rigorous maintenance routine was established, assisted by reference to engine-hour meters fitted in the cabs. In 1988 the diesels used £3.20 of fuel per trip and had a four-minute Llanberis turnround; this compared with an average of £51.00 and 30 minute turnround for steam. There are no hidden operating costs for the diesels, ash disposal being a particular bug-bear of steam operating. They carry sufficient fuel for a day's work.

To crew the diesels, the railway offered volunteers from existing footplatemen willing to undergo conversion training a bonus for driving both types of locomotive. There was some initial reluctance but once a man had qualified getting him back on steam was 'like pulling teeth', Rogerson said, the clean,

Top: No 3 *Wyddfa* in the early 20th century. A small amount of draught proofing has been added to its cab. *Judith Pettit Collection*

Left: No 4 *Snowdon*. Its paintwork is unlined. *Author's collection*

Below: No 5 *Moel Siabod* with one of the 1924 carriages. The device on the front of the control box to the left of the loco relates to train movements. *G. Alliez/ Author's collection*

Above: **A works photograph of No 6 *Sir Harmood,* as delivered in 1922.** *Author's collection*

Right: **No 6 was renamed *Padarn* in 1923. The nameplate is longer than it need be so that it could be fixed using the same bolt holes required by the *Sir Harmood* plates.** *Valentine/ Author's collection*

Below: **No 7 *Aylwin* seen on 1 April 1959. Its smokebox door and chimney are painted silver. If its livery is the same as No 8's at this period then its cab and tanks are painted brown.** *J. A. Peden/ Author's collection*

lightweight open carriage that would be run on Lancaster bogies in preference to a full-size carriage in the peak season. Thanks to Tony Ellis, Aitchison's report to the directors dated 6 July 1911 survives. Under the heading 'carriage', he wrote 'Whilst in Wales [10-17 June] the carriage which had been repaired by Messrs Holme & King was returned', which leaves no room for doubt.

There has been some confusion about the number of carriages obtained in 1923. A report in the *Locomotive* states that there were three, Société Industrielle Suisse records, not seen by the author, apparently list four. In the earliest minuted reference to new carriages, 1 December 1922, Davies had 'suggested that the Swiss Locomotive Company might be invited to tender for the supply of two coaches ...' and on 14 April 1923, 'It was reported

that a formal contract had been entered into with the Swiss Locomotive Company for the construction of two new coaches ...' which seems unequivocal. Photographs of No 9 loaded for delivery are dated August 1923 although it and No 8 reached Llanberis too late to be used in the 1923 season. In common with the 1896 Lancaster stock, they had seating for 56 in seven compartments, plus up to three more in the guard's coupé.

Stabled outside throughout the year the carriage bodies did not receive the maintenance they deserved. Boyd said that rebuilding was started on 'a small scale' before the war, but gives no evidence and none has been found. A comprehensive programme that saw all the carriages fully enclosed and glazed was started in 1947. It took place in stages, probably in the light

Top: **No 8 *Eryri* in silver and brown livery at Llanberis in 1958/9.** *Colour-Rail*

Left: **No 5's brown livery was new when photographed on 13 April 1998. The paint did not weather too well and soon faded.**

Right: **Freshly repainted in black, No 5 crosses the Afon Hwch for the first time as it leaves Llanberis on 25 March 2000.**

Below: **Repainted black in 1997, No 6 made a fine image when seen on 29 March.**

of experience; perhaps the passengers were more likely to complain than they had been. Firstly, the coupé was partially glazed, then the saloons were glazed in between the doors before, finally, the doors were made full-height. Because the vehicle numbers are not visible in most photographs it is not possible to track the changes. It may be that some carriages went from being fully open to being fully enclosed in one move.

Aerials have been affixed above the front windscreens since 1996, and more recently, the guard's windows have been equipped with a hand-worked windscreen wiper; No 10 had two wipers from new. Equipment to play a pre-recorded commentary describing features along the line has been installed recently.

In common with the locomotives, the original carriage livery was not recorded. In 1933, Davies reported that four carriages had been repainted, red, grey, green and orange (p69). In 1937 Kidner said the carriage livery was red or grey. According to Boyd the 1923 carriages were painted red with white lining. A picture postcard posted in 1939 shows one of these carriages painted in a light colour without lining that might well be grey. The author guesses that the orange one was the first to be repainted.

In his 1951 edition, Morris wrote that the carriages were painted 'engine-green, unlined'; for a period later in the 1950s at least one was painted chocolate-brown and cream. By 1960 all had been painted 'cherry red and cream', a scheme that has been retained with minor variations to this day.

Some photographs from the 1930s show the carriages with a roundel in the centre panel although none are sufficiently clear to reveal any detail. In the 1980s plastic stickers carrying the

railway's name were affixed to the leading ends; some vehicles also had these stickers on the carriage sides.

The Lancaster open carriage was converted to be a works car, primarily for carrying water, coal and other goods to the summit, the conversion a consequence of the opening of the 1935 summit building. An account published in the *Liverpool Daily Post* on 2 July 1938 states that 'Roberts [the manager] has designed a special tank that lies horizontal on the steepest gradient to convey the water for domestic purposes. This takes 800 gallons every other morning, unless rainwater gathered in reservoirs en route [Halfway and Clogwyn] and at the summit reduces the requirements. The earliest photographs of the vehicle are in Morris's 1951 booklet; it was equipped with an enclosed caboose for personnel at its leading end, a 1 ton-capacity coal bunker and a demountable 400 gallon water tank. Initially (Boyd), the tank was stored at Llanberis during the winter. Boyd and Davies gave the tank capacity as 700 gallons. The wagon was subsequently modified to carry the tank at an angle to increase its capacity. By 1964 (Ransome-Wallis), the personnel cabin had been rebuilt. This vehicle invariably forms the first train of the day, carrying blockmen, only one since the loops at Hebron and Halfway were automated, and summit personnel to their posts as well as the summit supplies. Oil replaced coal as the summit fuel following the 1982 refurbishment. The availability of the 2006-built Hunslet wagon to carry the summit supplies in larger volumes has allowed this vehicle to be rebuilt again; it now has a larger personnel cabin and carries a mobile generator. Although it carries no number, it is No 1 in the carriage fleet.

The other open carriage is also said to have been adapted for works use during the 1930s. Boyd said that he saw it in 1946 but was only able to sketch it; his description does not fit either of the photographs taken by Morris or Ransome-Wallis. Morris,

presumably writing in 1950 and who travelled on and photographed a works train, did not mention seeing two similar vehicles so most likely it had been scrapped by then.

Carriage fleet numbers are now shown on the back of the vehicles, at shoulder height, on the platform side when loading at Llanberis. From the 1980s until c2001 they were painted on the front of the vehicle. The 1923-built carriages had their numbers, 8 and 9, and the railway's name painted on their solebars but this probably only lasted until they were repainted. At some stage, perhaps during the 1950s rebuilding programme, the carriages were renumbered, the Lancaster carriages becoming Nos 2-5 and 8 and the 1923-built vehicles Nos 6 and 7. The East Lancashire Coach Builders Ltd carriage is No 10; its maker's number is GM1229.

Although the four-wheeled wagons were used on construction trains the SMR promoters also had expectation of freight traffic. The long-removed sidings at Waterfall and Hebron must have been for this purpose. The expectation failed to materialise and now only one of the wagons survives. Only two had been useable by the early 1930s (Boyd) and the last one was derelict when Morris saw it in 1950, a statement he repeated in 1960. However, a photograph shows it in use, complete with brake, in 1956 (p82). By 1964 (Ransome-Wallis), it was 'used for many purposes'. It is not known when its brake was removed. Originally, the wagons were numbered in their own sequence.

In the workshop an ambulance bogie is used when a carriage bogie is removed for maintenance. The timber frame, clearly of some vintage, was replaced by a steel frame in 2009.

After 2001 the railway reverted to a standard green livery for its locomotives as illustrated by this photograph of No 2 taken on 1 August 2007. By the same date No 4 had accrued red lining.

Top: **Nos 3, 6 and 2 on shed on 12 June 2009. It may be a standard livery, but the lining is different on each loco.**

Middle: **Shortly after delivery, on 20 August 1986, No 9 was photographed before it had been named.**

Botom: **No 9 *Ninian* at the summit on 18 August 1989.**

Top: **No 10** *Yeti* **had been painted in a revised livery when photographed on 8 March 1998. Its wheels had been removed for maintenance.**

Middle: **When it was photographed in June 1992, No 11 had not been named but its regular driver had personalised it to a small degree.**

Bottom: **Still nameless, No 12 was photographed on 1 September 1992. It was named** *George* **on 21 June 1996.**

Top: **No 12's purple livery was new when photographed on 24 March 2000, but it only lasted a short time before the standard green was restored.** *Author*

Middle: **Railcars Nos 21 and 22 had not been commissioned when they were photographed on the new sidings on 22 July 1995.**

Bottom: **The elevation and plan of the Lancaster carriages.** *Author's collection*

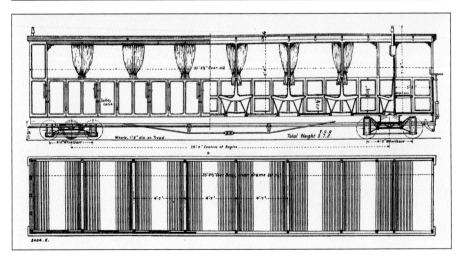

Top: **No 3 with one of the Lancaster carriages, as built.** *Commercial postcard/ Author's collection*

Above: **The carriage nameboards did not last too long, whether because they deteriorated in use or because they were deemed to be a hazard in strong winds is not known. Loco No 5 is seen at Clogwyn with one of the Lancaster carriages in this condition in the 1920s.** *Author's collection*

Left: **Lancaster carriage No 3 at Llanberis after it had been enclosed. There were detail differences in the way that this work was carried out.** *Author's collection*

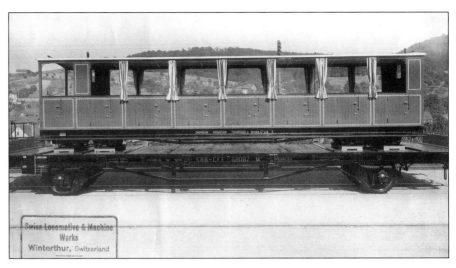

Top: **SIS carriage No 9 loaded for delivery in August 1923.** *SMR*

Middle: **When photographed with No 8 in 1938 one of the 1923 carriages retained a simpler form of lining and had also acquired a roundel in the centre of the bodyside.** *Valentine/ Author's collection*

Below: **Now numbered 7, one of the 1923-built carriages was seen passing the loco shed propelled by No 10 on 20 August 1986. The first BES-funded siding is in the foreground.**

Top: This photograph of No 4 at Clogwyn in August 1969 provides a glimpse of one of the carriages painted chocolate brown and cream. *Edward Dorricott*

Middle: Delivered in April, carriage No 10 awaited commissioning when it was photographed alongside No 8 on 24 May 1988.

Below:
The first incarnation of the caboose built on the frame of the shortened Lancaster carriage underframe, photographed with No 2 *c*1950. The water tank is stored on a wagon that appears to be off-rail.
O. J. Morris

Right: **No 6 descends to Hebron on 3 September 1953, its train comprising a four-wheeled wagon and the caboose. The ensemble came to be known as 'the truck' regardless of its makeup.** *R. E. Vincent/ Publisher's collection*

Below: **With a later caboose, the truck returns to Llanberis in June 1974. The area behind the train has been covered in houses and the viaduct, left, obscured by trees. The siding built in connection with the summit connection work now occupies the foreground. Compare with the centre photograph on p97.** *Alan Bowler*

Top: **The 2006-built caboose in the loco shed on 12 June 2009.**

Below: **The plan, elevation and section of a four-wheeled wagon.** *Author's collection*

Bottom: **A works photograph of one of the four-wheeled wagons.**
Author's collection

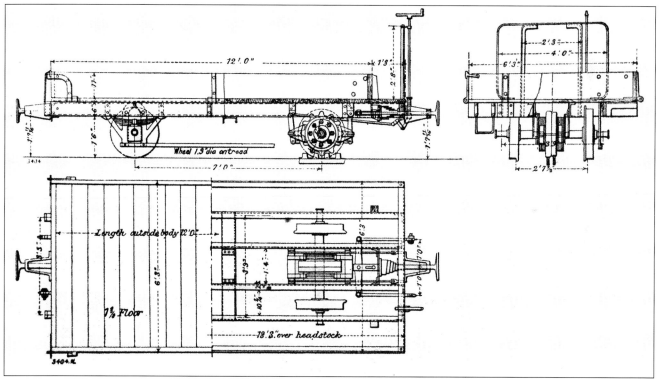

Above: **On 1 August 2007 the Hunslet-built bogie wagon was being readied for another trip to the summit building site.**

Below: **With the completion of the summit building works the Hunslet wagon is used to carry water and fuel to the summit. On 13 June 2009, it was seen near Halfway with 3000l of water and 1,000l of fuel. The loco was No 9.** *Andrew Hurrell*

Appendix 3

Profit, dividends and passengers 1895–2008

	Profit/Loss £	Dividend %	Passengers		Profit/Loss £	Dividend %	Passengers
1895	-	-		1959	10,294	8	
1896	-	-		1960	11,403	8	
1897	499	-		1961	12,809	12	
1898	475	-		1962	5,967	12	
1899	943	-		1963	2,922	12	
1900	292	-		1964			
1901	624	-		1965			
1902	N/A	-		1966			
1903	-615	-		1967			
1904	-304	-		1968			
1905	365	-		1969			
1906	N/A	-		1970			
1907	-97	-		1971			
1908	-453	-		1972	22,285	12	
1909	1,020	-		1973	21,485	14	92,280
1910	314	1		1974	18,879	5	
1911	1,136	½		1975	13,653	9	99,695
1912	446	-		1976	19,753	9	99,695
1913	1,582	-		1977	20,773	9	
1914	N/A	-		1978	22,183	10	
1915	605	-		1979	-39,630	6	
1916	206	-		1980	-37,246	-	
1917	N/A	-		1981	7,747	-	68,525
1918	-958	-		1982	4,009	-	
1919	4,624	-		1983	75,180	4	
1920	4,649	-		1984	104,948	6	86,541
1921	3,935	-		1985	78,719	-	76,539
1922	5,342	-		1986	11,615	-	85,204
1923	2,967	-		1987	34,791	-	88,933
1924	3,256	-		1988	13,764	-	97,578
1925	5,397	-		1989	98,560	-	120,826
1926	5,512	-		1990	73,388	-	122,172
1927	5,321	-		1991	-263,252	22½	
1928	6,532	-		1992	116,647	22½	
1929	6,418	-		1993	120,380	22½	
1930	4,773	-		1994	156,595	22½	
1931	3,750*	-		1995	209,579	30	141,790
1932	5,624	-		1996	152,402	30	156,944
1933	6,474	5		1997	157,699	30	147,981
1934	5,141	5		1998	129,776	-	141,000
1935	5,664	5		1999	192,707	-	
1936	5,633	5		2000	N/A	N/A	
1937	6,263	5		2001	N/A	N/A	
1938	6,469	5		2002	N/A	N/A	
1939	4,955	-		2003	N/A	N/A	
1940	-1,881	-		2004	N/A	N/A	130,657
1941	338	-		2005	N/A	N/A	140,948
1942	1,503	-		2006	N/A	N/A	131,069
1943	1,500	-		2007	N/A	N/A	126,732
1944	1,411	-		2008	N/A	N/A	123,703
1945	3,487	-					
1946	3,667	2½					
1947	4,572	2½					
1948	2,606	3					
1949	4,760	4½					
1950	4,342	4½					
1951	3,654	3					
1952	4,933	7					
1953	4,762	7					
1954	3,128	4					
1955	7,078	7					
1956	1,777	3					
1957	4,224	6					
1958	5,904	6					

Profit/loss and dividends extracted from the annual reports. Passenger figures extracted from various sources, including the Visit Wales website. The *Liverpool Daily Post* for 2 July 1938 stated that 'since the hotel was opened ... two record seasons have been enjoyed , as many as 40,000 persons having been conveyed ...'

Bibliography

Abt, R. S.; The Snowdon Mountain Tramroad;
  The Locomotive, 15 July 1931

Boyd, J. I. C.; *Narrow Gauge Railways in North
  Caernarvonshire*; Oakwood Press, 1981

'Indicator'; The Snowdon Mountain Tramroad;
  Railway Magazine, Vol 57, 1925

Johnson, Peter; By Rack to the Abode of Eagles – the
  Snowdon Mountain Railway; *Railway World*, March 1989

Johnson, Peter; *An Illustrated History of the Festiniog Railway*;
  Oxford Publishing Co, 2007

Johnson, Peter; *An Illustrated History of the Welsh Highland
  Railway*; Oxford Publishing Co, 2nd Edition 2009

Jones, Norman; *Snowdon Mountain Railway Llanberis*;
  Foxline Publishing, 1998

Jones, Eric and Gwyn, David; *Dolgarrog – an industrial
  history*; Gwynedd Archives, 1989

[Keylock, John]; Gowrie Colquhon Aitchison – AMICE, FCIS,
  1863-1928; *Welsh Highland Heritage*, No 8, June 2000

Keylock, John; Henry Joseph Jack (1869-1946);
  Welsh Highland Heritage, No 26, December 2004

Kidner, R. W.; *The Narrow Gauge Railways of North Wales*;
  Oakwood Press, 2nd Edition 1937

Morris, O. J.; *Snowdon Mountain Railway*; Ian Allan, 1951,
  revised 1960

Partington, John; The Snowdon Mountain Railway;
  Railway Magazine, Vol 1, 1897

Ransome-Wallis, P. ; *Snowdon Mountain Railway*; Ian Allan,
  1964, revised 1967, 1969

*Snowdon and the Snowdon Railway – a souvenir of
  Snowdonia*; Woodall, Minshall & Company, c1897

Snowdon & Welsh Highland Holiday Book; Snowdon
  Mountain Tramroad & Hotels Company Ltd, 1923

Snowdon Mountain Railway Llanberis offer for subscription;
  Hichens, Harrison & Company, 1985

Snowdon – Snowdon Mountain Railway Souvenir Brochure;
  Snowdon Mountain Railway, [2003]

Turner, Keith; *The Snowdon Mountain Railway*;
  David & Charles, 1973

Turner, Keith; *The Snowdon Mountain Railway*;
  Tempus Publishing, 2001

Turner, Keith; *The Way to the Stars – the story of the
  Snowdon Mountain Railway*; Carreg Gwalch, 2005

Williams, Rol; *Three Stops to the Summit – a history of the
  Snowdon Mountain Railway*; Cyhoeddiadau Mei, 1990,
  2nd Edition Carreg Gwalch, 1997

Above: **Dating this aerial photograph of the summit taken from a postcard posted in 1948 is not easy. After the war, SMR services to the summit were reintroduced in 1945, when there was no mention of a Nissen hut being placed over the terminal tracks as shown here. The hut undoubtedly originates from the summit's military occupation yet it seems unlikely that commercial aerial photography was carried out during wartime.** *Aero Pictorial Ltd/ Author's collection*

Right: **One of the posters commissioned from Ralph Mott to publicise the opening of the first stage of the 1935 summit building.** *Meg Davies Collection*

Index

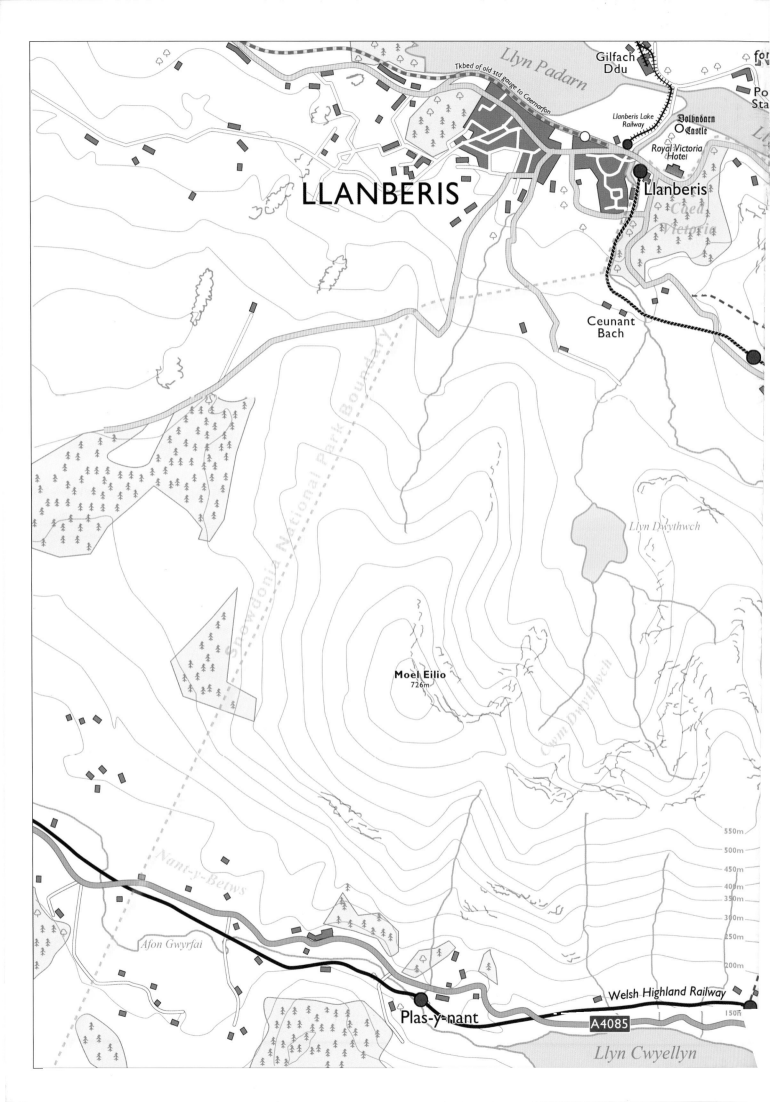